To John & Nancy

SCUTTLEBUTT

George E. Murphy

With best wishes

George E. Murphy
Aug 7, 2003

DORRANCE PUBLISHING CO., INC.
PITTSBURGH, PENNSYLVANIA 15222

To Pauline, my dear wife

Also by George E. Murphy:
It Didn't Happen on My Watch

ISBN # 0-8059-5998-X
Printed in the United States of America

First Printing

For information or to order additional books, please write:
Dorrance Publishing Co., Inc.
701 Smithfield Street
Third Floor
Pittsburgh, Pennsylvania 15222
U.S.A.
1-800-788-7654
Or visit our web site and on-line catalog at
www.dorrancepublishing.com

PROLOGUE

When an author begins writing a book, one of the first things he considers is "What should I name it?" While others probably already have a name selected at the outset, I didn't concern myself with this problem when I wrote my first book, nor did it worry me while putting this one together. I was primarily interested in getting my thoughts on paper; the name could come later.

When the time came to give this some consideration, I recalled some advice given to me by the first chief engineer I worked for back in 1943. His favorite slogan was, "Murphy, no matter what happens, always keep your bilges dry!" This remark didn't register with me at the time, but over the years I began to realize the old timer knew what he was talking about. He was seventy-four years old then, and had reactivated his license to come out of retirement to aid the war effort. He could have remained in retirement, or perhaps worked in the comparative safety of a defense plant or shipyard, but he elected to return to sea and risk his life in North Atlantic convoys while having the satisfaction of knowing he was doing his part.

Deeply rooted in his statement to me, a young nineteen-year-old third assistant engineer, was sage advice, far beyond ramifications of a small amount of standing water in various compartments of the vessel which must be pumped out to allow the area to dry and thus prevent rust and corrosion. It was his way of saying, "Keep your nose clean." In other words, "Treat the machinery with respect, maintain it properly, and remember, even the wipers, firemen, and oilers can teach you something" were some of the underlying thoughts covered under his slogan!

I considered this expression for a title until another thought entered my mind when I recalled a few instances aboard ship while serving as chief engineer, when a captain or mate called me to report a piece of equipment on the bridge had failed, either while in use or when attempting to start it. Normally, when an engineering type reports a malfunction to another engineer he will elaborate to some extent while reporting the problem, such as, "The bilge pump stopped while I was pumping out the forepeak," "I saw a bright flash come from the motor," "I could smell an electric burning odor coming from the motor," or "I heard a squeal and I think the pump may have seized."

When reporting a malfunction from the bridge, however, we would get, "Chief, the whistle won't work."

"Okay, I'll check it out. Can you give me some idea about the problem?"

"Yeah, I pushed the button and nothing happened!"

This would be the title, but I decided against it because it would be too difficult to explain, not to mention the embarrassment to those guys on the bridge.

Finally, while having lunch one afternoon with Tony Wong, about whom I have written in this book, I asked him for a suggestion for a name and he immediately answered, "Call it *Scuttlebutt*." After considerable thought, I agreed that would be it. Sea stories are a favorite pastime aboard ship, and rumors abound as well, and these fall under the category scuttlebutt; therefore the title.

When I published *It Didn't Happen on My Watch*, I expected some mild reaction from people in the marine industry, but was surprised at the comments I received from other readers across the country. Some were favorable, others not. Former shipmates whom I had long forgotten, steamship company executives, members of the armed forces, and long lost friends contacted me and felt compelled to tell me of their experiences at sea after having been reminded of them by the anecdotes in the book.

It also brought many comments from present and former shipmasters, chief engineers, and even children and other relatives of people highlighted in the book, many of whom thanked me for the complimentary remarks and stories about their fathers and uncles. Others expressed surprise that their fathers or uncles could have been guilty of some of the antics I wrote about!

Some captains expressed similar doubts, and one even accused me of fabricating some of the tales I told about them, alluding that captains would never behave as I wrote. Also, I didn't confine my remarks or unfavorable stories to captains and mates, but treated chief engineers and assistant engineers equally.

I recently attended a meeting of a group of captains, many of whom I knew, and when introduced to one I didn't know, he made the remark, with a touch of sarcasm, "Show me any captain on any coast who hasn't heard of him!" I smiled at this, knowing my remarks about captains in the book had prompted his reply, but I didn't gain any sense of satisfaction from it because I had written about them with tongue in cheek and no offense meant.

I was also critiqued by two captains for an error I made in a story about *Rules of the Road* when I described a collision situation in the Sea of Japan in which I labeled the wrong vessel as privileged instead of burdened. One quietly informed me of the error, explaining the *Inland Rules* which applied to the situation. The other captain sent pages of *Rules of the Road* with yellow highlighting throughout illustrating my error in various collision situations! He also took exception to my definitions of master, captain, and commander as I referred to them in the text and the glossary of the book. To this end he sent photocopies of pages taken from several dictionaries defining the terms.

A few United States Coast Guard personnel felt I had damaged the reputation of their service which struggles annually for enough appropriation to fulfill its mission and to recruit new enlistees. I referred them to the last paragraph in the coast guard chapter in which I explained my reasons for my attitude and that I had every praise for that branch of the service in its endeavors and that my only gripe was with the Marine Inspection Offices.

I like to believe that my complaints and criticism bore fruit, because in today's American flag merchant marine a large number of inspections previously carried out by coast guard personnel have been delegated to surveyors of the American Bureau of Shipping, a position I advocated in the book.

When the book was finally published in 1995 I enjoyed a sense of accomplishment. Whether it was successful or not didn't matter to me at that point. I had fulfilled a desire of telling my story plus many other incidents I had heard about during the forty-three years I was with United States Lines.

The anecdotes related here are follow-ups of some from my earlier book as well as new ones which I learned about from many readers and former shipmates.

THE OFFICE

World headquarters of United States Lines for many years was located at Number One Broadway in New York City. It was a prestigious address because during the company's glory years of pre-World War II and directly thereafter, lower Manhattan was the shipping center for the North Atlantic passenger and cargo trade to Europe. Most major shipping companies had their home offices in the area — companies such as Moore-McCormack, Grace Line, Robin Line, Farrell Lines, Cunard, White Star, and French Line, to name a few. Most had their passenger ship ticket offices in this area while their freight operations were located elsewhere in the city or across the Hudson River in Hoboken, Weehawken, and Jersey City, New Jersey.

Number One Broadway housed our passenger department in an ornate, tiled lobby at street level. Upon entering, a prospective passenger was directed to one of several counters over which was a splendid sign indicating first, cabin, or third class. Inlaid in the floor was a huge brass compass with an arrow indicating north, the exact direction of which was occasionally questioned as to its accuracy by some ship's engineers who wished to create a stir! Overlooking the lobby was a huge balcony which held various other offices needed for the many details in issuing a ticket. At times, during an occasional makeover of the lobby, many company officials would submit their bid to gain one of the offices on the balcony because it was an ideal spot for "doing company business," not to mention the choice view of the goings on in the busy lobby. Huge murals were painted on the walls, which also added to the splendor. The lobby of Cunard Line, located a few doorways north on Broadway, was also a showplace, with huge murals and elaborate ticket booths. Although these buildings now house a bank and a post office, they are protected under the New

York City Landmarks Preservations Commission and their décor must remain as it was during those earlier years.

Across from Number One Broadway lies the old Custom House, and next to this is located the Bowling Green, used by early residents. Bowling Green is the site where, in 1626, Peter Minuit, direct general of New Amsterdam, dealt with the Indian tribe which "owned" Manhattan Island to reach one of the greatest real estate bargains ever pulled off in the country.

The first structure built at One Broadway, in 1648, was a tavern. This was most appropriate because, after all, a shipping company which employed sailors would someday occupy the space and sailors have a reputation to uphold. At least the early ones were known for their love of grog, and it was here the first martini was created, it is rumored!

The operations department of United States Lines was located on the fourth floor of One Broadway. Here could be found the engineering department, deck department, stewards department, purchasing, insurance and claims, and vessel personnel offices.

The engineering department occupied a corner office which looked down on Battery Park, an excellent location for viewing the formations of many ticker tape parades. This huge office held eight desks with plenty of room to hold the office Christmas party, birthday parties, and other celebrations, and often it didn't really require much of an excuse to hold one!

The building was built early in the century and contained huge windows whose glass was full of flaws such as wavy lines, air bubbles, and other irregularities. Looking south toward New York Bay, one could get a wavy view of the Statue of Liberty, Governor's Island, and the Verrazano Bridge.

One morning, my boss, Dick Bower, was standing in the middle of the room looking in that direction and remarked, "I see the tanker, *Esso Massachusetts* is coming up the bay."

Tom Wilhelmsen, one of our port engineers, glanced up from his desk for a moment to view it, and then looked once again, and realizing he could barely make out the hull of the ship, remarked, "How can you read the name on that ship? It's barely visible!"

"It's my keen eyesight," Bower replied.

I peered out the window, as did another port engineer, Charlie Higgins, and we agreed with Tom, there was no way Bower could read the name on that ship. Charlie then walked over toward Bower and stood next to him, peering out the window, and said, "Let me stand where you're standing, Dick."

"You can't stand here; I'm standing here!"

"I want to stand exactly where you are."

"Charlie, there is only room for one guy to stand here. You stand there because I'm standing here!"

"I don't want to stand there; I want to stand where you are!"

I spoke up, "This is the dumbest conversation I've ever heard between two grown men!"

Tom, now realizing Bower could be using the wavy lines in the glass as a telescope, dialed Bower's telephone in his office, which was located around the corner from ours.

"That's your phone ringing, Dick," Tom said.

Bower abandoned his spot on the floor and left to answer the call. In the meantime, Charlie took over the spot and could easily make out the ship's name due to the wave in the glass. A moment later, Bower returned, "They had hung up by the time I got to the phone!"

Seeing Charlie standing in "his" spot, Bower laughed and called us a bunch of bastards, but promised to get even.

• • •

Tony Wong was another United States Lines port engineer who had previously gone to sea as a chief engineer in the company. He, like the others, welcomed the opportunity to come ashore and give up the seagoing life, to be able to be home nearly every night at a reasonable hour, and to make the countless days at sea just a memory.

He entered the office one morning a little earlier than usual, just as I returned to my desk with a cup of coffee. He had just pulled out his chair from behind his desk and started to sit down when I heard a loud tear!

"George, I just split my pants down the middle. What'll I do?"

"Let me see if Marie King has arrived at her desk yet. She always has a needle and thread in her drawer," I said, laughing as Tony stood there with his boxer shorts peeking out from the torn middle seam.

Marie was the secretary to the Steward Department, and her desk was just outside our engineering office. I left the office and found her just arriving and told her of Tony's plight. She was a fine lady and said she'd be happy to sew his trousers. I returned to tell Tony that she would gladly sew them; all he had to do was to remove them and bring them out to her. At this point he was seated deeply into the kneehole of his desk.

"I can't take them off and carry them out there in my underwear. I won't have any pants on!"

"Well, she's not going to sew them for you in place!"

"Will you bring them out to her?"

"Yeah, okay, I guess I can do that for you."

He slipped out of the trousers and handed them to me and then stayed seated deeply into his desk. Realizing the potential for a good laugh at his expense, I handed them to Marie and then went to see the vice president of operations, Ken Gundling, and to tell him of Tony's plight.

I asked him to call Tony on the phone and tell him to come to his office at once, that it was urgent, but to give me enough time to return to my desk. When I returned to our office his phone was ringing.

"Engineering, Tony Wong."

Tony listened for a moment and then, muffling the phone, turned to me. "It's Mr. Gundling. He wants to see me right away. What'll I do?"

"Tell him you can't come right away; you don't have any pants on!"

"I can't tell him that!"

After a slight hesitation, he blurted, "I'm sorry. I can't get to your office right now, Marie King has taken my pants from me! I mean she's working on them—they ripped!"

Tony listened and then hung up, turned to me, and said Gundling would come to see him. A minute later, Gundling arrived with his secretary and a file clerk, both young girls, and they began to engage Tony in a conversation while he was still deeply seated behind his desk in his underwear. After a good laugh, Gundling and the two girls, Cathy and Marie Ferrante, left the office and Marie King walked into the office holding his newly repaired trousers and handed them to him with a big grin!

Tony turned to me and said, "George, this was your idea. I'll get even!"

In today's office environment this sort of horseplay would not be tolerated due to sexual harassment rules, but it was fun while it lasted!

• • •

On another morning in our same fourth floor office, I opened the large window behind my desk and settled down with a cup of coffee when Don Kadlac entered. He chatted with me as he proceeded to lift the light plastic cover from the typewriter which was located directly behind me and placed the cover on the windowsill. Just as he began to type, Tom Wilhelmsen opened another large window in the opposite wall allowing a strong draft of wind to sweep through the room which scattered papers and picked up the typewriter cover and swept it out the open window. Don and I watched from the window as it floated downward like a wild kite heading for the sidewalk below. It struck a pedestrian on the head and he looked upward to see where it came from, and saw Don and me laughing!

Don asked, "What do you think I should do?"

"Tell the guy to pick it up and hold it for you, that you'll be right down to get it," I replied.

"He might be mad!"

"Well, we have to get the cover back."

"Hey, mister, hold it for me. I'll be right down," Don shouted.

I replied, "Don't worry, Don, I'll be right here if he gives you any trouble!"

"Yeah, from four floors away. Thanks!"

Frankly, I didn't care if he got the cover back or not; I just wanted to see if he would do it! In a few minutes, Don appeared on the sidewalk and I watched as the guy gave Don a lecture. Don kept nodding and then entered the building and returned to the office.

"Now, that wasn't so bad was it?"

"Are you kidding? That guy was wild!" was all he would say.

• • •

A few days later Bower had to go to the west coast for a meeting with the west coast shipyards and returned ten days later. When he entered the office we asked the usual questions about the meeting — shipyard billing rates agreed upon, availability of various yards to accept our new ships, etc. — but while discussing these issues, Bower appeared to have a bewildered look about him.

"Anything wrong, Dick?" Charlie Higgins asked.

"Nothing too important. I'm just trying to figure where I spent $6.50. I worked up all my expenses and can account for everything except $6.50."

"Maybe you had a drink at the airport," Tom Wilhelmsen suggested.

"Yeah, I did, but I counted that."

Knowing that Bower watched the company expenses in our department very closely, not to mention his own expenses for going to work each day, and seeing that this bothered him, I reached into my desk drawer and withdrew a pad of blank receipts and handed it to him.

"Here, boss, make out a receipt for it."

"I can't do that. That isn't right!"

"We do it if we are on company business and can't account for a small amount; it's not always possible to get receipts," Charlie added.

"Well, I don't. That isn't exactly honest. I'll just try to remember where I spent it," he said and left the room to return to his office.

He returned in five minutes with a stern look on his face. "George, let me have one of those blank receipts!"

I handed the book to him. He tore out two pages, threw the book at me, and left our office without saying a word. Charlie, Tom, and I looked at each other and just smiled.

On another occasion, Charlie and I were leaving to go to lunch when Charlie stuck his head in Bowers' office and told him we were going to lunch and he wanted to know if we had a "sponsor." Seeing the opportunity for a good laugh, Charlie said, "Yeah, with Dutch."

"Dutch, from Todd Shipyard?" Bower asked, as he was putting on his topcoat.

"No, Dutch Treat!"

Bower made an immediate U-turn, removed his coat, and called Charlie a smart ass. Bower then ate a sandwich at the company lunch counter in the lobby!

• • •

One man for whom I enjoyed working was the assistant superintendent engineer, Robert Lurye. He was a graduate of New York State Maritime Academy from the late twenties and a classmate of Charlie Higgins. He was a good boss and instilled in the port engineers his sense of integrity and honesty. If we experienced a problem in our job of husbanding a ship during repairs, he told us not to minimize the problem to him, but lay it on the line so as to prevent any surprises later from upper management if the ship's departure were to be delayed.

Another of his axioms was, if we had any doubt about releasing a ship to go to sea, would we, as the chief engineer, take it out under the same conditions? If our conscience said yes, then let her go. On a few occasions we delayed a sailing because of his teaching.

His own honesty paid off one time while returning home to Staten Island from the office. He and one of our port captains, Bill Howard, were crossing the Goethals Bridge in Lurye's new Buick when they were stopped by a Port Authority cop at the Staten Island end after paying the toll.

Striding up to his car, the officer asked, "Do you know what the speed limit is over the bridge, mister?"

Lurye replied, "Officer, I'm a college graduate and I work with numbers all day in my job, and yes, I can read the speed limit on the sign. If you're going to give me a ticket, just do it and let me get home. I've taken all kinds of crap from VPs and general managers all day long in my job and I just want to get home, kick off my shoes, make a big martini, and sit down and relax, so just do your job and let me go home!"

The officer, obviously irritated by his attitude, replied, "Okay mister," and left to go to his patrol car to get his ticket book. He seemed to be gone a long time, but when he returned he said, "You know something, mister, you're lucky. I just came on duty and I forgot to bring a pen with me and I can't find one in the patrol car, but while I was looking for one it gave me time to think. The last thing you need right now is a ticket; what you do need is that martini. I admire your honesty, mister, so I'm letting you go with a warning! Drive carefully, obey the speed limit, and enjoy that drink!"

Needless to say, Lurye was overwhelmed by this and could only sputter, "Yes sir. Thanks!"

He was shaking his head in disbelief as he drove away saying to Bill Howard, "I don't believe it. Just because he couldn't find a pen!"

Howard remarked, "Hell, I had a pen in my pocket he could have used if he had only asked me!"

Lurye's reply to this statement cannot be printed in this book!

• • •

Lurye purchased his Buick while our operations department offices were located at Pier 62, at the foot of Twenty-third Street in Manhattan, prior to our move to Number One Broadway. He was extremely proud of his new car and used it to commute from Staten Island to the office each day and would not hesitate to explain its grandness to anyone who asked.

The port engineers had a standing reservation each noon in the Cornish Arms Hotel dining room with a different contractor hosting each meal, but Lurye would not drive his new car the seven blocks to the hotel, opting instead to take a cross-town bus. Each lunchtime conversation would start by Lurye and it was always about another feature of his new car which he hadn't discussed earlier, such as a light going on when he opened his glove compartment, or trunk, or the mirrors over his sun visors, or when he pulled out the ash tray, and he would always end the sentence with, "I didn't have that on my last car!" We listened to his daily ravings patiently because, after all, he was the boss!

After two weeks of this, as he was about to describe another feature of the car, one of the port engineers, George Low, a mild-mannered, middle-aged man who had the disposition of a saint and one from whom we had never heard a harsh word, picked up his dinner knife and fork and slammed them down onto his plate, making a loud noise which drew the attention of all the other patrons in the restaurant.

"I'm fed up with hearing about that _ _ _ _ car of yours. I can't take it anymore. You've ruined our lunch for the last two weeks. Give us a break!" This tirade was sprinkled with expletives we couldn't believe came from such a meek, mild-tempered man as George! Lurye slumped down in his chair and, after giving some thought to George's remarks, never mentioned the car again at lunch! Later, out of earshot of Lurye, we thanked George!

The following Saturday Lurye had driven to the office to catch up on some paperwork while Al Roland, another of the port engineers, and I were working in New York winding up work on the ships we were handling. Upon completion of my work I returned to the office and began talking to Lurye about my ship. When he learned I was finished with the job, he asked if I would do a favor for him and ride in the backseat of his Buick while he drove along Twelfth Avenue so I could attempt to determine the cause of a couple of squeaks he could hear while driving. We went to his car and I climbed into the seat and he began driving along the road while I listened carefully. I could hear no squeaks so he asked me to ride in the trunk where he thought I might be able to pick up the noises. Being the newest port engineer in the office, I wasn't about to refuse him, so I said I would. I climbed into the trunk, he closed the lid, and we got underway once again. He drove northward on West Street and turned into another United States Lines pier at the foot of Thirty-fourth Street, the pier where Al Roland's ship was berthed. After turning around on the pier, he started southward toward Twenty-third Street, but was followed by

Roland who had just finished his ship and was returning to the office. He stayed behind until Lurye pulled into Pier 62 and then parked next to him. Roland began talking to Lurye about his ship when Lurye walked around to the rear of his car and unlocked the trunk, allowing me to climb out.

Roland stood there, his mouth open with a dumbfounded look, and then spoke. "Now I've seen everything. The boss won't even let you ride in the inside of his new car. You gotta ride in the trunk?" While I explained, he made some snide remark about what some guys would do to hold their job! At least Lurye was happy because I located the cause of the squeaks!

• • •

A couple of months later, I asked him if I could apply a bumper sticker on his rear bumper to advertise a Boy Scout jamboree to be held in New Jersey a month later. I was a councilman for my local Boy Scout troop and was assisting in the planning for the jamboree.

"Are you kidding? Not on my new car. Like hell!"

The following day I parked next to his Buick, and on a whim I glued the sticker to the bumper. The following morning when he arrived in the office, he was furious! He had been stuck in stop and go traffic the night before while entering the Holland Tunnel on his way home when he was rear-ended by the motorist behind him. When he got out of his car to examine the damage he saw the sticker and then claimed the collision was my fault because the guy behind him was trying to get close enough to read the printing on the sticker!

Fortunately, his car wasn't damaged, but I spent the next couple of hours in the parking lot removing the sticker!

• • •

For some unknown reason Al Roland always seemed to be the port engineer who would get the plush job whenever one arose. He would just be in the right place at the right time when the company was to undertake a new project, try out a new experiment for the Maritime Administration, test out some new equipment a vendor may be attempting to sell to the company, etc.

One Monday morning he called the boss from home to tell him he would be unable to come to work in the office because he had cut off the fingertips of his right hand with his lawnmower. His family doctor had pronounced him unfit for duty for the time being and he would not be ready for work for at least a week. In the meantime the SS *American Lancer*, one of our new container ships, had sent a message to the office that it was having a vibration problem with a forced draft fan, and the chief engineer had determined it was due to a bent shaft. The ship had just left New York for the Far East with a full load of cargo, and nothing in the world would delay this ship, if management had its way. The next incoming ship, a sister ship of the *Lancer*, fortunately had the fleet's spare shaft aboard and was due in New York in a few days.

Management made the decision to inform the incoming ship to have the spare shaft ready to go ashore immediately upon its arrival at the pier and have it picked up by a port engineer, who would transport it to Newark Airport in his car, purchase a first-class ticket to Los Angeles, and put the shaft aboard the same flight as "accompanied baggage." It was not unusual for port engineers to do this; we had done it many times before.

The port engineer, with shaft, was to meet the *American Lancer* at the pier in Los Angeles, hire a shipyard gang to install the shaft, and stand by to supervise its installation, which would go on concurrently with the vessel's cargo operations. With luck, the shaft installation would be completed at the same time as cargo operations and the vessel would sail on schedule. The only drawback to this plan was there was a good chance the ship would arrive in Los Angeles long before the port engineer and shaft arrived! If this were to happen, the ship would sail out of Los Angeles on schedule and the port engineer and his cargo would fly to Honolulu, the ship's next port, and await the arrival of the ship and install it there.

Dick Bower called me into his office and told me of the plan and also told me I was to be the port engineer to ride with the shaft! I went home that night and informed my wife of the difficult assignment I had just been given, that the chance of my meeting the ship in Los Angeles was extremely remote due to scheduling, and that I would be "forced" to fly to Honolulu and await the arrival of the ship which would not be due in for five days.

She appeared to do a slow burn as I told her of this, and she said, "You're too cocky. Something will happen to burst your bubble; wait and see!" A few days later I went to the office and told the boss everything was ready for the ship's arrival the next morning. My bag was packed and I would be ready to go. A few minutes later his phone rang. It was Roland. "Hi Boss. Al Roland here. The doctor just gave me a 'Fit for Light Duty' slip, so I'll be ready to go to work tomorrow. Do you have anything for me? The doctor told me just to be sure to keep my hand elevated." Bower looked up at me, smiled, and said, "Roland, there's no lighter duty than just flying in an airplane. Be ready to go to Los Angeles and perhaps Honolulu tomorrow morning!" And he went on to explain the details of the trip to Roland while I stood there with my mouth wide open!

"Mr. Bower. I don't believe what I just heard," I blurted out.

He went on, "You be ready to drive Roland to the ship in the morning. Take the shaft off the ship for him — I don't want him lifting anything heavy with that bad finger — and drive him to the airport and assist him getting on the plane!"

The following morning we got to the ship and the crew had the shaft all rigged and standing by the gangway ready to go ashore. They had tied a big red ribbon around it with a sign, "Have a nice trip, Mr. Murphy!" *Yeah*, I thought, *talk about rubbing it in.*

As it developed, Roland and the shaft missed the arrival in Los Angeles and had to go on to Honolulu where it was installed. Roland returned to the office a few days later sporting a magnificent tan, but with his hand still elevated. He then said to me, "I still have to keep my hand elevated until the doctor tells me it's okay to lower it."

After studying the grin on his face and looking at the elevated hand, it seemed to me that his middle finger was elevated a lot more than the other fingers on that hand!

• • •

The early beginnings of United States Lines date back to 1893 when a corporation was set up as International Navigation Company. Several years later, it was renamed International Mercantile Marine Company, which included White Star Line, among others. When I joined the company in 1943, upon graduation from Massachusetts Maritime Academy, several other steamship company names were painted on the windows of the Operations Department at Pier 62, North River, New York, in addition to United States Lines. Companies such as Roosevelt Steamship Company, Panama Pacific Company, Coastwise Line, and American Pioneer Line were all part of United States Lines at the time.

Other companies were also familied into the corporation, but they were not steamship companies: a trucking company named Pier 59 Trucking Company, another named Pier 61 Trucking Company, and still another named Chelsea Trucking Company. These companies consisted of one truck each, an old Mack with solid rubber tires, which I would imagine were vintage early thirties. Their only operating route was twelve blocks long, from Twenty-third Street (Chelsea Piers) to the General Post Office at Thirty-fourth Street to pick up mail destined for Europe.

Another company which was part of the operation was a carpenter shop called Chelsea Ship Repair, whose facilities were located on the company piers. Their function was to shore up cargo in the holds and on deck of the freighters to prevent it from shifting in the heavy weather of the North Atlantic. When necessary they also would construct a walkway over any deck cargo which the company might be carrying on the ship's deck, to allow safe passage at sea for men to check the steering gear aft on the ship.

My boss, Joe Cragin, superintendent engineer, had his office on Pier 62, and it was directly opposite the office housing the other port engineers in those early days. One port engineer, Jack Lee, was a Scotsman who enjoyed a little nip of Scotch now and then an he knew Cragin kept a bottle in the deep drawer of his desk. Soon after Cragin left at 5:00 P.M. each day, Jack would duck into his office and take a nip from the bottle in Cragin's unlocked desk.

Cragin, a non-drinker, kept the bottle for hospitality reasons, but could never figure why the level was slowly going down. He called the Chelsea Ship carpenters and asked them to install a lock on the deep drawer, which they did the following day, and he now felt his booze was secure. Little did he know!

It didn't take Jack long to figure this one out. He found that by merely removing the drawer above the locked one, he could reach down into the drawer and lift the bottle out! When Cragin saw its level still falling, he accused the Chelsea carpenters of providing duplicate keys for the lock to the thief! He then went to a hardware store and purchased a new lock and kept both keys, but much to his chagrin, he kept losing whiskey.

At his retirement party years later, we discussed if we should put his mind at ease and tell him what happened to the booze, but everyone decided not to. Let him stew over it!

Another small company was also making a living off United States Lines—the company painters. A crew of about twelve men were on the steady payroll and were used to paint the rooms of crewmembers and officers on the ships. In those early days, the walls of the ships in the crew quarters and passageways were painted steel, and with a fleet of forty to fifty ships, the painters were kept quite busy. When a passenger ship came into port, they were assigned to that ship until it left. When paint rollers came on the scene the painters balked at using them because they speeded up the painting considerably and the painters could see their need slowly fading, especially since the fleet was being upgraded with fewer but faster ships whose bulkheads were constructed with a prefinished, fireproof plastic coating which never needed painting!

Still, in another small section of Pier 62, could be found four seamstresses whose work consisted of repairing any tears in curtains, blankets, spreads, sheets, etc. from the ships. At the end of each trip, the chief steward would gather together any of the above which needed mending and turn them over to the women for repair.

Any linen from the passenger ships which was found damaged was replaced with new and the damaged pieces repaired and used aboard the freighters. I recall some captains and chief engineers complaining about their curtains not matching the two portholes in their rooms! One would have a green curtain, the other a red one. This prompted some captains and chief engineers to have their wives sew new curtains at home and then install them themselves, if they were to remain on the ship for any length of time!

One interesting note about the seamstresses: If a first-class passenger spilled something and caused a stain, or burned a hole in a blanket with a cigarette, the steward promptly replaced the blanket and turned the damaged one over to the seamstresses at the end of the voyage. They examined it and attempted to dry-clean it to remove the stain. For the blanket with the burn they attempted to invisibly mend it. If neither operation proved to be successful, the blanket was cut into quarters and trimmed to eliminate the stain or burn, and each side then hemmed, thereby creating four new small blankets. These were then turned over to the kennel keeper for his use in providing comfortable bedding for his charges.

Often, the company had a surplus of these small blankets and made them available to us in the office for twenty-five cents each! I purchased a dozen and gave them to the veterinarian in my town who treated my family cat! He was proud to tell pet owners that if their cat or dog had to remain overnight they would probably be sleeping on a blanket which had been previously used by the Duke of Windsor or the president of the United States!

• • •

One other entrepreneur who gleaned a living from the company, although not a member of the United States Lines family of companies, was a man whom we dubbed the Pillow Merchant. He would drive a long trailer truck onto the passenger ship pier on arrival day of either the SS *America* or SS *United States* and set up his equipment to clean a certain amount of pillows from the ships. The chief steward would have a number of pillows already removed from the passenger staterooms and ready for him to pick up.

He would then insert them into one end of the trailer where a machine would slit open the pillow casing, dump out the down feathers into a receptacle, and then send the casing through a dry-cleaning process. In the meantime the feathers were being sanitized and fluff dried and upon completion would be stuffed or blown into the clean casings and a machine would then sew the end up and stuff the clean pillow into a paper envelope to be returned to the steward. Because of the nature of this process he was also dubbed Mr. Fluff and Puff!

THE SHIPS

Sea Trials

Most seagoing personnel never get the opportunity to take part in a vessel's sea trials unless they have been assigned to the ship prior to its delivery, and then usually only the senior officers might have the opportunity. As a ship nears its completion date, the shipbuilder, regulatory bodies, owners, labor unions, and vendors make plans to conduct a series of trials to prove the ship has been built to owner's specifications, and that it fulfills all other requirements according to law, union agreements, etc.

Sometimes a trial is held alongside a pier where some machinery is tested, such as cargo handling equipment, and subsequently at least one sea trial is held where the vessel leaves the builder's yard for the first time and goes to sea to test the remainder of the machinery and equipment. Occasionally, the yard may conduct its own builder's trial prior to the owner's trial. During the official sea trial for acceptance, all machinery is put through its paces: main engines, boilers, and auxiliary machinery such as evaporators, generators, pumps, steering gear, etc., with at least one representative of each manufacturer present whose equipment is aboard during the test.

In addition to owner's representatives, aboard are members of the United States Coast Guard Marine Inspection Office, American Bureau of Shipping Surveyors, United States Public Health inspectors, union representatives, at least one each from the unions represented on board, machinery manufacturers' representatives, vendors from paint companies, and shipyard personnel from nearly every department in the yard.

15

All clamber aboard early in the morning of the trials carrying a suitcase containing toiletries and a change of clothing. While the ship might have been designed to hold a crew of about thirty-eight men, it must accommodate over two hundred individuals during the trials for at least two days, so sleeping space is at a premium. The shipyard will set up cots in passageways, staterooms, storerooms, and any place else where these extras may be accommodated.

Many veterans of previous sea trials will rush aboard early and stake claim to one of the officer or crew bunks by placing his suitcase on it; however, more than once has an old timer been frustrated when he dashed to the captain's or chief engineer's room to claim the bunk, which is usually a little wider than the others, only to find the shipyard has not yet installed a mattress! Often one doesn't know who his roommates might be until the ship is ready to leave the pier.

Soft drink companies, such as Coca Cola or Pepsi Cola, often set up coolers in various compartments, on the bridge, and in the engine room with a supply of paper cups and furnish soda free of charge as a publicity stunt and an opportunity for free advertising. Soon after leaving the shipyard, maintenance men from the yard will visit each toilet and shower and install a roll of toilet paper and a showerhead, and leave a few cakes of soap and a supply of towels.

Manufacturers' vendors can be found in every area of the ship, tuning up their equipment and preparing for their scheduled time test. On one occasion, aboard the SS *American Lancer* during her trials, the representative of the sewage disposal system manufacturer had been boasting about the efficiency of his unit, claiming that the effluent from it was so pure and environmentally safe that one could drink it! His unit could not be tested the first day of the trial because it had to be demonstrated while its holding tanks were full, thus the second day was scheduled for the test, after the tanks were assuredly full from the many people aboard. On day two, while he was tuning up the unit, he started one of its pumps, and an obnoxious smell arose from the disposal. He withdrew a sample of the effluent from a test line and it was a deep brownish nauseating color. He immediately shut the system down, and after a quick examination of the unit discovered one of the yard electricians had mistakenly wired the effluent pump to run backward. In the meantime, two wags from the yard were standing by, each holding a paper cup and telling him they were waiting to see him drink it as he had boasted!

A great deal of coordination and planning go into the trials so that numerous tests can be conducted simultaneously without too much confusion. On another trial I attended the cooks were testing the galley equipment and had just completed cooking two huge turkeys in the ovens and had placed them on a stainless steel table in the galley for carving. Just at that moment, a worker entered the galley carrying a stepladder which he intended to use to clean the grease filters over the range. As he turned, his ladder knocked the turkeys from the table onto the deck. At that moment the ship was making a hard left turn at full speed as part of it performance trials, causing the ship to heel slightly to port. The two turkeys, already in motion from the fall, continued their travel across the deck and crashed against a cabinet on one side of the galley. The cabinet door swung open from the collision and an open bottle of detergent dumped on the turkeys! I grabbed one turkey and a cook grabbed the other and we lifted them onto the table.

We stared at each other for a moment and then broke out laughing. We grabbed a fistful of paper towels and wiped the turkeys clean and covered them, where they remained until they were carved an hour later and served for dinner!

Trials continued on through the night with the respective vendors demonstrating their equipment. Upon completion of a test of a particular piece of equipment its vendor would retire to his sleeping area for a few hours sleep. Prior to leaving the shipyard, I had looked into several rooms to learn where various vendors and inspectors were billeted and found every room and compartment fitted with cots from wall to wall!

I got up early the following morning to witness a test and went into one of the rooms to use the head. The evening before, the room had been filled with bodies spread throughout the room, but that morning I found the room empty, except for one man asleep on a cot. However, the passageway outside the room was littered with sleeping bodies on cots. At breakfast I asked one of the men who had started out the evening before in the room why it had emptied during the night and he replied, "Are you kidding? That one guy you saw left in the room this morning came in last night, turned in, and immediately started snoring. It became louder as the evening wore on and soon the first guy got up, folded up his cot, and left the room to set up in the passageway. A moment later, another guy did the same, and soon after the rest of the room cleared out! One man even complained the snoring woke him in the next room, while another complained that the middle of the night was a hell of a time to be testing the ship's whistle!

At the completion of the trials, just prior to docking in the shipyard, a yard worker will go to all the showers and remove the showerheads, much to the chagrin of many men who hadn't yet found time to take a shower. This was standard procedure on each trial because often the ship would return to the pier and several of the heads would be missing.

• • •

A story is told about a retired official of Newport News Shipbuilding Corporation who was riding through the Virginia countryside with his wife one afternoon when they decided to stop at a small country restaurant for lunch. This official had worked in the shipyard during the construction of the SS *United States*, the flagship of United States Lines, and was very familiar with many of the officers and crewmembers of that ship, having worked with them for the three years during its construction.

As he and his wife settled in for their meal, he noticed a paragraph on the menu which gave a little history of the restaurant, plus another paragraph which mentioned the chef of the restaurant was formerly the chef on the SS *United States*. Having known the chef on the ship, and also knowing that he was a distinguished German "Chef de Cuisine" named Otto Bismark who had passed away a few years ago, the official asked the waiter if he could meet the chef.

The man who appeared from the kitchen began to laugh hysterically when he saw the man from the yard. The two knew each other, and after a good laugh the official explained to his wife that the chef was the owner of a delicatessen in Newport News who supplied the food aboard the SS *United States* during its many trial trips!

As he explained, "You gotta do what you gotta do to make a living these days!"

I had never met Otto Bismark, but knew of his reputation from company officials. One time while the SS *United States* was tied up at Pier 86 in Manhattan, an electrical contractor was working in the ship's galley doing some wiring to an electric grill. I had reason to call the contractor from the office on the telephone about a pending job I had for him on an incoming ship which I was handling as port engineer. When the operator on the ship picked up I asked her to connect me with the galley. Otto Bismark answered "Galley" in a strong, guttural voice with a distinct German accent.

"I'd like to speak with Joe Hennessy. He's an electrician working on the electric grill in the galley, please."

"Who is dis?"

"My name is George Murphy, port engineer."

"Do you know who I am? I am the chef. I am not an errand boy. I do not run all over ship looking for people!"

With that the phone remained silent. I did a slow burn while contemplating my next move when a voice came on the phone. "Is there someone on here?"

"Yeah," I replied, "I was hung up on. I'm trying to reach the electrician who is working on the electric grill. This is the office calling."

"This is the galley utility. I'll try to find him for you."

A moment later, I was talking to Hennessy.

"Joe, if you see that German chef around there, rewire the switch to the grill so he gets knocked on his ass when he turns it on the first time, will you?" And then I told Joe the purpose of my call. When we later met on my ship he remarked he had never heard me so angry.

Many people in our freight sales department held steady accounts which could be depended upon for repeat business, but they still had to go out and hustle to fill the ships. Many of the goods carried were of a seasonal nature, such as Christmas toys, summer and winter clothing, and foodstuffs, so these were regularly carried for repeat customers, year after year.

The salespeople could not rest on their laurels, however, and were under constant pressure to gain new customers. Often a shipper would call to ask if we could ship an irregularly shaped piece of freight which could not be loaded into a container. In our break bulk days this would have to be evaluated before the company would commit itself.

Such was the case one time aboard one of our Lancer-class ships when the company accepted a brand new bright red fire engine. Too large to fit into a container, it was loaded aboard and stowed on a hatch cover just behind the midship house, at the base of the port side king post. On these vessels each king post in reality was a smokestack for a boiler in the engine room, and what appeared as a single smokestack in a profile of the ship was a ventilator room holding supply and exhaust fans for various compartments in the ship.

Upon completion of loading, the vessel left New York bound for the Far East. While the ship transited the Panama Canal the chief mate had the crew wash down the ship while the ship was in Gatun Lake, a freshwater reservoir which feeds the locks of the canal. This is a routine procedure carried out on nearly every ship because it gives the crew a chance to wash off months of accumulated salt from spray taken aboard in the course of each voyage. The wash down then gives the deck department an opportunity to touch up the paintwork on deck.

A day after leaving the canal the weather was fine—no wind, no spray, sun shining brightly, an ideal day to paint. The exteriors of the king posts (smokestacks) had held an accumulation of soot on their exteriors as a result of the engineers blowing the boiler tubes each day. While most of the soot was blown clear each time, downdrafts often caused a lot of it to adhere to the paintwork of their exterior. This loose soot had been washed off during the Gatun Lake wash down, so the chief mate decided it was an excellent chance to paint them.

He sent an AB aloft to rig a boatswain's chair to a grab rail at the top of the king post. After rigging it, the man dropped a line to the deck where another man tied a gallon of aluminum paint on the line and the man above heaved it upward to where he sat. When the bucket arrived, the man in the chair found the paint can still had the cover on it. How smart, he thought, leaving it covered so it wouldn't spill on its travel aloft!

He carefully removed the cover with a screwdriver, and while reaching for a paintbrush he inadvertently upended the can of paint. The entire contents of the can spilled downward, spreading out as it traveled thirty-five feet to the hatch cover. It landed squarely on the cab of the fire engine and spread out to nearly completely cover the entire forward section of the truck with aluminum paint!

They broke out all hands of the deck department and started to attempt to clean off the paint before it had a chance to dry, but their efforts were in vain. They borrowed kerosene from the engine room plus any other solvents they could think of to assist in the cleanup. The steel of the truck was extremely hot from having been exposed to the sun for so long that the paint dried almost instantly when it landed. The boatswain chewed out the AB, the chief mate chewed out the boatswain, the captain chewed out the chief mate, and the office chewed out the captain for attempting to paint aloft with such a valuable cargo directly beneath.

When the fire engine was discharged, the consignee made out an exception to his cargo and filed a claim to have the truck exterior refinished. A circular letter from the office followed to each ship, without mentioning the name of the ship, warning the crew to be more diligent when painting on deck. While no names were mentioned, everyone in the fleet knew within two weeks the name of the ship and the captain.

THE SHIP'S A FEEDER!

The cooks who worked on United States Lines ships were members of the National Maritime Union, and many attended union-sponsored cooking schools where they developed skills as butchers and bakers and for the most part were quite capable of putting out a dinner which would equal the product of many good hotel kitchens. For many, their skills were limited by the lack of some of the finer seasonings and cuts of meat which were available ashore, but still many brought their own spices and flavorings aboard, knowing they were unavailable on board. Most took great pride in their work and appreciated a kind thank you for the full-course Christmas or Thanksgiving dinners which were served, or for the birthday cake for an unsuspecting crewmember.

There were other cooks aboard, however, who were not members of the steward department, such as the first assistant engineer, Tom Rollings, aboard the SS *American Jurist* where I served as chief engineer. On that ship the steam supply line to the high pressure turbine was made up of several sections of six-inch diameter steel pipe bent in gentle curves flanged to each other and ran from the boiler to the inlet side of the turbine. At the turbine inlet flange was located a spectacle flange which is a flat piece of steel three quarters of an inch thick in the form of a figure eight, sandwiched between two flanges of the same diameter. It was constructed with an opening on one side the same diameter as the pipe through which the steam passed to the turbine, and its other and was solid steel. Its purpose was to be used as a blank during a hydrostatic test of the steam pipe during the vessel's annual machinery inspections. It was unbolted and swung around until the blank area was lined up with the steam pipe, thus preventing the high-pressure water during the test from entering the turbine. Once the test was completed it was unbolted and swung around so its opening once again lined up with the steam flow. During normal steaming conditions, the protruding side was exposed to the atmosphere and with the steam passing through it at approximately 800 degrees, it made an ideal heating surface. Enterprising engineers on board utilized this heated area by cooking bacon and eggs on it.

I had always noticed how clean and shiny its surface was instead of the usual dull color of steel under high heat and wondered why, until I discovered during a visit to the engine room a crew member polishing it with a piece of emery cloth in port.

The following day, at sea, I entered the upper engine room to hang up some laundry for drying and caught the pleasant aroma of bacon and eggs cooking, and the galley wasn't even open yet. I went below and found Rollings and his oiler and fireman enjoying an early breakfast! I was upset at first because their attention was focused on breakfast and not the operation of the steam plant, but this group had always stood a very efficient watch so I said nothing. Besides, the aroma got to me and I joined them for breakfast!

On another occasion, aboard another ship, I was called on the phone at eight o'clock in morning by the captain, John Hart, while at sea.

"Chief, what the hell is going on with that second assistant engineer of yours? He's got the chief steward all upset! He's ordered a dozen scrambled eggs for breakfast. No man can eat that many at one sitting! Find out what the hell is going on, will you?"

I had already finished eating breakfast and was seated at my desk when I got the call, so I strolled into the officers' dining room and spoke to the second assistant, Walter Wood. Walter was always feuding with the chief steward, who was a naturalized Greek and spoke poor English.

"Woody, what's going on with the eggs?"

"I ordered a dozen scrambled eggs, chief—three for me, three for the second mate, three for the engine cadet, and three for the deck cadet. Three times four is twelve."

He continued, "At 0730 I called the second mate from the engine room and asked if he was planning on ordering three scrambled eggs as he usually did and he replied that he was. I then asked him to check with the cadet what he wanted and he also said three scrambled. I then checked with the cadet on my watch and he also said scrambled, so we decided whoever got to the dining room first would order a dozen, but don't let the steward know they are going to be split four ways, and watch him blow his top!"

These four men always ate breakfast together because they got off watch at the same time. I just shook my head and went to see the captain and explained it to him, but during this time while the issue was being discussed, and the eggs finally served, breakfast period was over and the mess man told the steward he would have to be paid overtime for serving the four men beyond the meal hour and the captain blew his top!

Captain Hart liked to sleep late each morning and hated to be disturbed before he was ready to wake up. He had blown up at the steward earlier that morning and now blew up again when he learned the mess man wanted overtime.

OIL SPILLS, OOPS!

I hardly believe there is a marine engineer who has not been involved in a fuel spill sometime during his career. Before the environmentalists began calling attention to the pollution being caused by fuel spills, crews were constantly overflowing their tanks during fuel transfer aboard ship or while fueling their ships to capacity, particularly when under pressure from the office because the price of fuel was so cheap in a particular port.

One of the engineers assigned to my ship once overflowed a settling tank while in a German port and the fuel spilled out the tank vent on the main deck and then ran overboard when it reached a freeing port. We estimated the spill to be about one hundred fifty gallons, or nearly four barrels. Oil spills are always described in gallons when reported by the press to highlight the quantity; one hundred fifty gallons is much more impressive than four barrels! The spill accumulated along our port side and clung there without any movement. Fortunately, at least for us, it was at night so we started our main circulating pump, the discharge of which was just at our waterline, and it shoved the entire spill under the pilings of the pier to which we were tied up, and there it lay until we left the port at midnight.

On another occasion we had a similar spill, but this was on the offshore side of the vessel and the spilled fuel lay in the middle of the shipping channel, again at night. While we contemplated our next move, a huge passenger ship began moving up the channel, going astern. In order for it to tie up to its pier heading outbound, it had to turn in a turning basin several hundred yards before reaching its berth and then proceed backward up the channel.

When its stern reached the oil spill, its twin propellers chewed the fuel spill into a huge emulsion which soon dispersed so that by morning no trace of fuel was evident.

Many years later, while working as a port engineer, I was in Long Beach, California, and had a few hours to spare so I paid a visit to one of our ships, the SS *American Scientist*, which was working cargo. I visited the captain and chief engineer to see if there was anything I could do for them during their brief stay in port, before they left on their voyage to the Far East.

While talking to the chief engineer he received a phone call from the second engineer in the engine room. "Chief, I just pumped a few barrels of fuel overboard; the tank level gauge is broken!"

He informed me of this and we ran to the pier where we saw an oil slick slowly spreading on the surface of the water at the ship's side. The flow of fuel had stopped, but the slick remained and was spreading. We didn't have an office in Long Beach at that time, but we used a shipping agency for handling the ship's business. I called the port engineer of the agency, Hugh Brown, and informed him of the spill and he said he would get a recovery team and cleanup crew on the scene immediately.

Within twenty minutes a truck arrived at the pier and a short time later a boat came alongside with cleanup gear. A floating boom was placed out on the water from the boat and rigged to surround the slick and keep it contained, and a pump on the boat began sucking the fuel from the surface of the water. Their quick response was critical because only a few hundred yards away was a marina which held several yachts, and every one had a white hull! I had visions of United States Lines being sued by every one of them.

Unknown to me, the law required our agency to also call an oil spill response group made up of river police, environmentalists, city police, and a few others, for a total of eight people. Suddenly this group converged on the scene to observe the cleanup. One of them, a burly man, bellowed, "Who's in charge here?"

I replied, "I am, sir."

"What happened?"

"The crew was transferring fuel on our ship and the tank level indicator malfunctioned and the tank overflowed slightly."

"You call that slight!" he bellowed.

"Yes, I estimate it to be about a hundred gallons."

"What steps are your taking to clean it up?"

"I called our agent and they dispatched the cleanup crew you see here with the truck and boat."

"Alright. We have to sit down somewhere and discuss this more thoroughly. We take spills seriously here in California. Where can we go?"

I invited them to a room off the starboard side of the bridge where it was quiet and contained a table and chairs. I asked if they would care for a cup of coffee and he said, "No way. We're here on serious business. We frown on ships from New York coming into our port and spilling fuel into our harbor."

I then wanted to ask if it had been a ship from a west coast company would it have made any difference, but I thought better of it and kept quiet. My burly friend seemed to be in charge and wore three stripes on his shirt and was addressed as sergeant by everyone. I assumed he was taking charge of the investigation, to the obvious relief of the others.

He settled in at the table opposite me, and then a man seated next to him took out a pad and pencil, ready for the questioning.

"What's your name and title?" he asked.

"George E. Murphy, port engineer."

Turning to his writer, he repeated, "George E. Murphy, port engineer."

"Company name and home port?" he continued.

"United States Lines, Incorporated, New York, New York."

"United States Lines, Incorporated, New York, New York," he repeated to his writer.

Everyone else remained silent while the interrogation continued, with the sergeant repeating my answers to the writer.

I realized how serious a fuel spill was, but had to contain myself and keep from smiling as I answered and then listened to him repeat it to his crony seated beside him.

Meanwhile, I was hoping Hugh Brown would soon arrive to assist me in this inquisition because he more than likely knew all these men and had probably dealt with them before, while I was a New Yorker in the midst of a hostile group.

After a few more questions, the sergeant said, "Alright, Mr. Murphy, by the powers vested in me by the City of Long Beach, California, I hereby issue this summons to you, as a representative of your company, to appear in Long Beach Municipal Court on Monday morning at 9:00 A.M. to answer the charges I have brought here today. Sign here, please."

"I'm sorry, sergeant, I cannot sign any documents without the advice of counsel. I don't have the right to commit my company to any form of legal action; therefore I refuse to sign your document," I said.

He replied, "That don't matter, Murphy, consider yourself served with this summons," and he thrust it at me. I accepted it and sat back for a moment to read it.

He then said, "I hereby declare this hearing dismissed. Thank you, gentlemen."

I shouted, "Not yet, sergeant. I have a few questions I need answered for my company. Please sit down, gentlemen."

He sat down with the others and I removed my pocket notebook and started interrogating the sergeant, stalling for time.

"Your name?"

His writer spoke up, "He's Sergeant Jones."

"First name?"

"Joseph" the writer repeated.

Turning to the writer, I asked, "Are you Sergeant Jones, or is he?"

"I'm Sergeant Joseph Jones," the sergeant blurted out.

"Then why is he answering my questions? I'm asking you!"

"Shut up, Charlie. I'll answer him."

After a few more useless questions, the door opened and in walked Hugh. He said hello and shook hands with all present, calling each by his first name, and living up to my expectations.

"Where do we stand, George?" he asked.

"I was just issued a summons by the sergeant, Hugh," I said, handing it to him to read.

He studied it for a moment and then said, "You've done it again, sergeant. You scheduled a court hearing for an oil spill on a Monday. The judge told you twice before that he changed the court calendar and is hearing traffic violations on Mondays now and oil spill violations on Thursdays. He's gonna chew you out again!"

"Oh, migosh, you're right, Hugh. Murphy, gimme that summons back!"

"I'm afraid I can't do that, sergeant. I've been served. I'll have to consult with my people in New York about surrendering it!"

Hugh then said, "Sergeant, can I speak to you outside?"

The two left the room and returned in about five minutes. Hugh then asked me to step outside.

"George, the sergeant is willing to forget the whole incident if you'll surrender the summons to him. He will destroy it and the oil spill incident will be over, providing the cleanup is completed at U.S. Lines expense."

I agreed to this and that ended it, particularly since the company had planned to pay for the cleanup anyway. I gave the summons to Hugh, and when we returned to the room the entire group had left by another door and was gone from the ship. Talk about saving face!

• • •

United States Lines at one time painted the hulls of their ships a gray color, but soon changed it to black when, after the war, several ships suffered fuel spills which would dribble down the side and mar the beauty of the ship. The ships' engineers were happy to see this change because any traces of fuel on the black hull would not show after a spill.

During World War II a gray, oil-streaked hull was a characteristic of Liberty ships. The fueling system of some was such that each double bottom and deep tank had to be filled by pressure from the fuel-filling hose, while others were built with deep tanks which could be filled from the hose and their valves in the engine room and those valves to the double bottoms could be opened at the same time. The fuel would then gravitate to the double-bottom tanks and when they were filled, their level would only be at the same level as the deep tank, with no danger of an overflow. Unfortunately, the two Liberty ships I served on during the war were of the pressure-fill type, so I must admit my ship had its share of spills.

• • •

Often, the chief engineer is called upon to transfer fuel from one tank to another to trim the ship to a more even keel or reduce the drag on the hull if it is too deep by the stern as a result of cargo discharging and loading. This is not always possible, however, if the ship's tanks are full as a result of fueling to capacity.

This occurred one time on my ship, the SS *Pioneer Ming*. Our captain had gone to the officers' club in Hawaii where he had been chatting with a naval architect who had told him he was instrumental in the design of the *Pioneer Ming*, a mariner-class ship constructed by the government. The architect told him this type of vessel operated most efficiently at sea when on an even keel, so the captain told the chief mate, Bill Atterbury, to be aware of this fact so that the ship would be loaded for the homebound trip from Japan to Long Beach, California, as close to an even keel as possible. Atterbury explained this would not be practical because the ship was to fuel to capacity in Long Beach, and the bulk of the bulk of the fuel would be loaded in forward tanks, thus putting the ship down by the head leaving port. Also, past experience had indicated the ship operated most efficiently with a four- to five-foot drag. The captain replied that he would deal with that problem when we came to it, but for now load it as he said. Atterbury attempted once more to convince him, but his argument fell on deaf ears.

A few weeks later we were leaving Yokohama for Long Beach and the ship's draft was within two inches of an even keel, a good job by Atterbury in keeping the captain's orders.

Upon our arrival in Long Beach we fueled to capacity as scheduled, with every tank chock full. The third mate went down on the pier after fueling and just prior to sailing to read the draft. We were six feet by the head, just as Atterbury had predicted. When the third mate informed the captain of the draft he was told to read it again, he must have made a mistake, and to take Atterbury with him to verify it! There was no question about it, and the captain came rushing to me. "Chief, how soon will you be able to transfer fuel?"

I explained it would be at least three days because after a full day of steaming we would consume 600 barrels, and we could not move any appreciable amount then because it was necessary that we draw a small amount from all eighteen tanks on board in order to take the head off them, lest their fuel expand as we entered the warmer waters approaching Panama and spill out on deck. Day three would be our first chance to trim the ship, so at that time we filled our day tanks from the forward-most tank, which only changed the draft a few inches. Aboard the ship every eighty tons of fuel consumed changed the draft by one inch!

We continued using fuel from the forward-most tanks, but when we arrived at the Panama Canal we were still three feet by the head! Panama Canal regulations prohibit a passage through the canal by any vessel unless it is at least on an even keel, so any passage by our ship was out of the question upon our arrival. The canal authorities would permit our passage only if we consented to a tugboat escort through the entire length of the fifty-mile passage. The cost was about five thousand dollars! Our agent would not commit to that amount until he got the okay from our office in New York, which told him to go ahead and get that ship through at any cost.

Needless to say, when we returned to New York the captain had a lot of explaining to do and was given a trip off for his stubbornness!

• • •

I had an embarrassing incident one time in Yokohama over the quantity of fuel on board the *Pioneer Ming*. Our Far East run always scheduled two stops at Yokohama, the first to discharge the inbound cargo after which the ship left for ports in Korea, and then returned to three other Japanese cities—Kobe, Nagoya, and Shimizu—before returning to Yokohama.

United States Lines shared a huge fuel tank in Yokohama with Pacific Far East Lines in order to have a supply of fuel available to each company when one of the ships needed fuel to get to our west coast where the ship would be fueled to capacity as explained earlier. During their voyages, ships for both companies would be fueled to capacity leaving the West Coast, depending on their loaded condition, and the excess discharged into the tank for storage. When a ship leaving Japan required fuel it would be drawn from this supply because fuel purchased from Japanese sources was prohibitively expensive.

Our Yokohama office contacted me in Kobe and asked how much fuel I had on board so they could plan on the amount I would require when we reached Yokohama. The figure I gave them was the amount which was showing in our logbook; however, I later took deep soundings of the tanks and when we arrived at the pier in Yokohama I gave the office a different number which varied from the original by about two hundred barrels, but which was much more accurate.

A runner from our Yokohama office contacted me and told me our office manager wanted to see me about the variation in figures. I went directly to his office and was greeted by a cute little Japanese girl, his secretary.

"Me chief engineer, SS *Pioneer Ming*. Mr. Yamamoto call me from ship. You understand?"

"Hai," she replied, meaning yes, and brought me into his office where he was seated behind a large desk.

"Mr. Yamamato, me chief engineer, *Pioneer Ming*. I want to explain why more fuel on ship than logbook. I take soundings after I give fuel number at Kobe and get true number of barrels on ship. You understand?

"Hai."

"Fuel soundings more accurate. True figure. Logbook number wrong. You understand?"

"Hai," and then he burst out laughing hysterically, and said, "In other words, you have fuel up your sleeve like all chief engineers, correct?"

I did a double take when I heard this, "You speak perfect English!"

"I should, I'm an American like you are. I was born in California and attended the University of Southern California and was recruited by United States Lines right out of college ten years ago and was trained in our west coast offices before this duty here! I wanted to see how long I could keep a straight face while you spoke broken English to me."

We enjoyed a good laugh and then we went to lunch together.

MORE ON FUEL CONSUMPTION

As I mentioned earlier, when serving as chief engineer aboard a ship which is one of a group of similar-type vessels, the company would compare the ships to each other in various departments. If one ship consumed more paint on deck for a given time than another, if one's feeding costs were greater than another, or, in my case, if one ship consumed more fuel than the others we were called upon to explain. For this reason I was always happy to remain in the middle of the group, neither too economical nor too expensive to operate my department.

The second assistant engineer aboard the SS *American Jurist* was a naturalized American citizen from Estonia, and proud of his heritage, so much so that it began to get on my nerves after a while. He complained about the construction of the ship, how uneconomical its machinery plant design was, the loss of heat through the boiler casings, not enough insulation on the main turbines, and many other things. "European ships are built much more efficiently than American ships. They are designed better, and will last longer," he would preach.

He also prided himself on being a better engineer than American engineers and always attempted to prove it by consuming less fuel on his watch than the other two watches. This irritated the other two watch engineers, because, practically speaking, his watch should have consumed more because of the extra activity carried out, such as blowing boiler tubes each watch and pumping the day's supply of fuel to the settling tanks from various other tanks throughout the ship.

I would stroll down to the engine room unannounced in an effort to discover his secret at different times of his watches, but could never find anything unusual. I even set a small piece of thread on the bypass to the fuel meter, thinking he would knock the thread loose if he were to crack open the bypass slightly, but it was never disturbed.

The ship had four huge built-in tanks for carrying cargo oil in bulk and the commodity most carried was tallow, which required an enormous amount of heat to keep it in a liquid state. Built-in thermometers would indicate the temperature of the tallow and it was controlled by opening and closing steam valves to the heating coils mounted inside the tanks. One evening on one of my surprise visits, I entered the shaft alley where the thermometers and steam valves were located and found the temperatures to be normal, but upon further examination I discovered the four valves to the heating coils turned off.

I said nothing to the engineer, but returned to the engine room a half hour after he was off watch and found the valves to be open again, enough to maintain the temperatures. I asked the engineer how the tanks were doing and he said, "The temperatures are right on the money, chief. As a matter of fact I haven't had to touch them at all this trip. The second assistant seems to have them adjusted just right each time I come down on my watch."

I repeated my trips to check the valves and after four consecutive days of finding the valves shut off on his two watches each day, I confronted him with my findings. He turned crimson when I asked why they were off and he mumbled something about he was afraid the temperatures might get too high and scorch the cargo!

He reasoned that as long as the cargo stayed at the proper temperature all day on the other watches, he could shut off the steam and then turn it on again just before he went off watch and the heat would remain the same during the shutoff period, thereby reducing the amount of fuel consumed during his four hours!

He quit his job upon our return to New York. I had to assume he could read my mind! I later learned from other sources that he had been closing in on the turbine throttle slightly to reduce the volume of steam admitted to the turbine but not enough to affect the revolutions of the propeller.

SHIPWRECK

One of our newly acquired vessels, the SS *Pioneer Muse*, ran aground in Okinawa in 1962 due to a navigation error. It had been steaming steadily at twenty-one knots when it slammed up onto the rocks, hard and fast. The engine room slowly flooded and the engineers found it necessary to secure the steam plant when they realized they could not keep ahead of the inrush of water, using all available pumps.

The captain eventually gave the order to abandon ship, so the crew rigged a Jacob's ladder over the bow and let it land to the rocks below while the crew slowly descended the ladder, taking some personal gear with them. With the engine room flooded, the ship eventually broke in half and the after end slowly sank while the bow section remained hard up on the rocks.

I had just stopped going to sea at the time and was in my first month of working in the company office when the casualty occurred. On the morning we received the word, our passenger ship SS *United States* was arriving at Pier 86 in the Hudson River and I was with my boss, Joe Cragin, superintendent engineer, riding to the pier to meet the passenger ship. I had been handling engine department personnel at the time, and one of my duties was to meet the passenger ships on arrival to square away any problems with vacations or relief personnel in the engineering department. While in the cab, I asked Cargin if it were true we had just lost a ship in the Pacific, and he growled at me, "Don't let me hear one more word about a ship sinking. Is that clear?"

For some reason I thought if he didn't want to hear about it, maybe the ship was lost through some error on board caused by the engineers. I later learned that was exactly what he was thinking. At this point no one in the office knew what had caused the loss of the ship and he wanted no rumors started!

The officers and crew of the ship were repatriated to Japan where, the following day, they boarded a flight to Kennedy airport which would arrive in New York about 10:00 P.M. Port Captain Bill Kolbe and I were sent to Kennedy to meet the crew—Kolbe for the deck and steward departments and me for the engineering department.

We had reserved a block of rooms at a motel at the airport to house the men for the night, our purpose being to hold the crew together until morning at which time a bus would transport everyone to our passenger ship terminal in Manhattan.

There their union representatives would be present to handle any grievances, our paymaster would pay them off, and additionally each would be presented with a check in the amount of five hundred dollars, a contractual amount agreed upon for anyone shipwrecked, regardless of the individual's losses.

When Kolbe and I arrived at Kennedy, we found a small crowd assembled in the gate area awaiting the plane's arrival in spite of the late hour. Parents, wives, and sweethearts were all milling around. When the plane finally arrived and the crew left the plane we attempted to corral everyone to keep them together to explain our plan to them, but it was pandemonium!

When the dust settled, we managed to herd them together and explain our plan. The motel rooms were assigned so that the two crewmen who had shared a room on board the ship would also share a motel room, making it easier for us to keep track of them, but many lived in New York and wanted no part of a motel room after what they had just been through!

I found one oiler who was clinging to a young lady about twenty years old and told him his room number and that he would be sharing the room with the fireman on his watch. They were standing near the cadet who was with his parents and his girlfriend, when the oiler announced, "Are you crazy? You think I'm going to spend tonight with the fireman when I got this lovely cutie to sleep with? No way, mister. I've been dating her for over a year!"

Of course we had no official jurisdiction over the officers and crewmembers; they knew that and that was the reason for his outburst. I glanced over at the cadet's parents and they were standing there horrified at the oiler's remarks! It went through my mind that they were probably thinking, "Goodness, is this the profession our son is entering and are these the types he will be associating with?" Most, however, took advantage of the rooms because of sheer exhaustion after such a long flight.

In the morning we gathered them together and onto the bus to Pier 86. There their union representatives, the paymaster, and many others were present, including the press to get their stories. We requested each crewmember to complete a claim form which held his name and an area to write in all the gear and equipment which he had lost due to the shipwreck. Some questioned the reason for the form when they knew they were entitled to only five hundred dollars, regardless of their claim, but we explained this was a requirement from our insurance company.

We collected the forms and were surprised at what some had written. Many claimed to have lost two or three Hart, Schaffner, & Marx suites valued at $275 each, three Stetson hats valued at $75 each, and many pairs of Florsheim shoes. These from men who had never been seen in anything except dungarees! Another claimed to have lost twelve dozen pairs of ladies nylon stockings, "to further Japanese-American relations with Japanese girls," as he further wrote. Another even declared several set of ladies' underwear with a day of the week embroidered on each!

One engineer approached me with a minor problem. He had contracted with a Hong Kong tailor to make two suits for him on his previous trip to the Orient and was due to pick them up this voyage on the *Pioneer Muse*. As personnel director for the engineering department, I had held open two engineering jobs on the next week's ship just in case someone from the *Pioneer Muse* needed a job, so I was able to ship him out on that ship and he eventually picked up his new suits.

The men were paid off and received their shipwreck money. In the meantime, the United States Navy wanted to retrieve some of their cargo which was stowed in the forward holds in the section of the ship still aground on the island. They contacted Captain John Green, marine superintendent, who arranged for a portable generator to be installed on the deck of the ship and power supplied to the forward winches to enable the cargo to be discharged. After giving it some thought, Green decided he had better make the trip to Okinawa to personally oversee the discharge of the cargo. Some in the office wanted to call it a junket, a good chance to get out of town, but no one dare say anything like that to Green! Green made the trip and the cargo was discharged without incident.

A few months later, a visitor to Green's home in northern New Jersey discovered the bronze bell from the bow of the *Pioneer Muse* mounted in an elaborate wooden support in his backyard! Obviously his junket to the Far East was not a complete loss and served another "useful" purpose in addition to overseeing the cargo discharge! Of course, Green was thinking ahead; with the Chelsea Ship Repair Company just a doorway away from his office in New York, it was only natural that Chelsea would "volunteer" to construct the wooden support for the bell. At another time, Mrs. Green was attending an afternoon luncheon with other neighborhood women, when one lady mentioned she would like to obtain the name of a good carpenter; her husband had many small jobs requiring the services of one and Mrs. Green volunteered, "You should hire a company called Chelsea; they have good carpenters. They built our garage and back porch and did a very good job!" I never found out if the Greens stopped talking to each other after she let the cat out of the bag!

WHISKEY ABOARD

For many years, our passenger ship, the SS *United States* was on a steady, fast turnaround schedule between New York and England and France and was only taken out of service at Christmastime for her annual overhauls. On these occasions the ship would arrive in New York, disembark its passengers and any cargo from Europe, back load any spare parts which may have arrived in the company storeroom for installation during the shipyard period, and lay off the steward department personnel who were not required during the yard stay.

Crew members were granted permission years earlier to purchase liquor "out of bond" from licensed chandlers in the European ports as long as it was kept locked up aboard ship in a sealed locker and declared on the crew member's customs manifest before being distributed just prior to the ship's arrival in New York. This privilege was rarely abused by the crew, because the cost of good Scotch whiskey was quite reasonable in the United kingdom and crew members could stockpile it at home in preparation for the holidays.

On the trip prior to the shipyard period, however, not all the Scotch was declared! Many crewmembers had friends who worked in Newport News Shipyard and would arrange to bring in any number of bottles, undeclared, and sell them to them much cheaper than the yard worker could buy it ashore. In this manner yard workers had a chance to have holiday whiskey at a reasonable cost and the crewmembers could make a few extra dollars for the holidays. It was then up to the yard employee to smuggle it ashore. Such was the case on what was to be the last voyage of the SS *United States*.

After the vessel called at New York and passengers and steward department were gone, a few company officials and VIPs boarded and made the overnight trip to the yard—a short trip which was in reality a big party! The officers and remaining crew were informed at that time that the great ship had just completed its last voyage and was due for lay-up! Those crewmembers on board had an additional headache: In addition to soon losing their job, what to do with all the whiskey they had purchased for the yard workers? With any luck, they could make contact with them and get rid of it quickly, before the final day.

Unknown to these crew members, however, the shipyard had changed ownership recently and the new owners had been checking on the income for the yard from relatively little known resources such as scrap value for torn and ruptured steel from collision and grounding repairs, and until it could unscramble the vast complexities of these small bits of income, it informed all the workers that all lunch boxes, packages, automobiles, and trucks leaving the yard would be searched at the gate, and the guards would be assisted by United States Customs Officers to prevent undeclared goods from going ashore.

The workers then had to inform the crew that any deals for whiskey were off; no one wanted to jeopardize his job for a smuggled bottle of booze! To further complicate matters, the ship had just been secured to the pier when an army of customs searchers, rather crudely called "The Forty Thieves," began boarding to conduct a search for contraband!

Word spread quickly about the searchers, and crew members began pouring whiskey down the drains of their toilets, showers, and sinks, hoping to beat the ominous knock on the door by a searcher. When a few bottles were drained, they were rushed out of the individual's room and thrown into a waste receptacle in a public space so no one could be accused of having unmanifested contraband in his possession! Many crewmembers had used public spaces such as storerooms and lockers to stow their stock of whiskey so as not to be caught with it and thus did not attempt to recover it from its hiding place when the customs boarded.

Much of this was found by customs and seized, but of course they had no idea who was responsible. The usual penalty for this is a fine for the company, and if found on a person or in his quarters he is subject to a fine as well. A smuggling fine nearly always resulted in the discharge of the crewmember.

Today one may hear a rumor from a former crew member who wonders if the two or three bottles he had stowed in a ventilator room or air conditioning room or machine shop locker were ever discovered, or are they still there?

SCUTTLEBUTT

Only time will tell whether it's found someday by a worker refurbishing the ship as a floating restaurant, museum, or hotel or by a worker from a shipbreaker's yard! Rumors abound that there is still a lot of good Scotch on board if only one knows where to look!

41

SCUTTLEBUTT

United States Lines always provided its shipmasters with a case of Scotch whiskey prior to leaving New York on a routine trip to Europe. It was to be used for hospitality reasons such as a little libation for customs inspectors, public health officials, immigration officers, and other officials who may have boarded the vessel (including other company captains who may have been in the same port); however, this is not mentioned in the company rulebook!

Although these trips would last about five weeks, the marine superintendent would often wonder how twelve bottles could be consumed when the vessel called at only four or five European ports. Of course, it was out of the question that any captains would take any home while the ship was in New York. Some captains were even known to give a bottle to the chief engineer occasionally for entertaining underwriter surveyors, coast guard inspectors, or American Bureau of Shipping surveyors.

I recall one time aboard the SS *American Jurist* where I was serving as first assistant engineer, the chief engineer, Norman Jones, was asked to take a job ashore as a port engineer in Baltimore upon our arrival in New York. He accepted it and I was promoted to chief. It would be my first trip as chief and I was quite excited about it.

The ship was undergoing a coast guard biennial inspection while in New York, so I asked captain Jim Knowlton for a bottle of company Scotch to ease our way through the inspection. I believe I caught him off guard with my request because his first reply was, "Oh, I don't know. I only have six bottles left; I think the BR (bedroom steward) has been nipping on my whiskey when I'm out of my room!"

I could believe him because the BR did appear to be under the influence at times, but I asked what that had to do with my being given a bottle, and I believe he said it because he was at a loss for words when I asked him!

"Where did you keep the whisky, that the BR found it? I asked.

"It's kept in my locked clothes locker. I'm talking about the open bottle I have to keep hiding; right now it's in my underwear drawer!"

He opened the drawer and removed the partially filled bottle.

"Well, it looks like he didn't find this one. The level is still at the edge of the label where it was when I hid it. Take this one, chief. This should be enough for what you want," and handed the half-full bottle to me.

Before I could complain about this juvenile treatment he added, "Be sure you return what you don't use!"

I bristled when he added that and left his office in a silent rage and returned to my office where the inspectors were waiting. I told them about my conversation with the captain and they said, "Chief, I think under these circumstances we should make sure there isn't any left to return. What do you think?"

"Absolutely. I'm glad you suggested it," and they consumed the rest of the whiskey.

I later returned the empty bottle to Knowlton and told him the circumstances which brought about the empty bottle and how embarrassing it was for me.

"Well, I would have given a full bottle to you if I had know there was more than one inspector," he said, and then went to his closed locker and handed a full bottle to me.

"For future use, chief. No hard feelings, and there's more here if you need it. No hard feelings?"

We shook hands and got along fine after that. I remained chief on the ship for the next three years while he was captain.

• • •

Immediately following World War II, United States Lines wasted no time in resurrecting its peacetime cargo operations. Its overseas offices had to be restaffed, in some cases due to personnel casualties in war, plus the addition of new employees to solicit cargo from European manufacturers who were attempting to resume their peacetime shipping. The same conditions existed in this country as well—former employees returning from the armed services and new people joining the ranks.

One such individual was a man named Captain Paul Revere Smith, a former navy officer who had previously been employed briefly in the company before being called to active duty. The company was eager to get into the transport of bulk cargo oils, commodities which were good revenue-earning products, and Captain Smith was named head of this project.

Many ships had built-in tanks which were designed for carrying fuel, but were easily converted to the carriage of cargo oils by merely blanking off the piping inside the tanks to prevent contamination of the cargo should a crew member open a wrong valve from the fuel system. Another minor requirement was the installation of thermometer wells to monitor the temperature of the cargo, some of which would require a little heat from the steam coils installed in the bottom of each tank.

Smith came aboard the SS *American Jurist*, where I was serving as first assistant engineer, and informed me he had been placed in the position of overseeing the conversion of the tanks as well as overall manager of the cargo oil detail for our entire fleet. Since the ship did not yet have the thermometer wells installed and we were to be the first ship to carry this type of cargo, the successful carriage of which would mean a lucrative contract for the company from the shipper, it was necessary that the cargo be delivered in good condition.

He repeated this to me at least three times while we were in the engine room. He told me to come with him to the shaft alley, whose bulkheads formed the inner sides of the tanks where the cargo would be carried. Walking up to one area, he placed the palm of his hand on the steel and said, "Feel this steel, Murphy, and tell me what temperature you think it is. Until the thermometer wells are installed this will be the only way you will know the temperature and they will not be installed until you return from this trip."

I placed the back of my hand against the area where he had felt and told him it was about eighty-five degrees.

"Where did you ever learn to tell temperature with the back of your hand? Use your palm, like I did."

"I learned you get a truer sense of warmth with the more sensitive area on the back of your hand than with your palm. Engineers have been doing this for years!" I blurted out.

"Well, you're wrong about the temperature of that steel. It's easily about ninety-two degrees."

He continued, "Let's go into the engine room and feel an area which has a thermometer and I'll show you what experience will prove."

We entered the engine room and he rushed to a generator in operation and grasped the lubricating oil line from the cooler to the generator bearings. While holding the pipeline in his left hand his right hand had blocked the face of the thermometer in the oil line so I couldn't read it.

"Feel this pipeline, Murphy. What do you think this temperature is?"

I felt it, again with the back of my hand, and said, "This is about one hundred eleven degrees."

"No, no, it's much hotter than that. It's about one hundred twenty-five. Now, let's take a look!"

Removing his hand from the thermometer, he squatted down and read the temperature. "This shows it as one hundred ten. Let me have your flashlight!" I handed the light to him and he verified the temperature.

"Are you sure this thermometer is correct?"

"Yeah, it was just calibrated last week."

"Well, young man, you see what I mean by experience. Just keep a close watch on those tanks when the oil is loaded."

I should have left well enough alone, but didn't want him to get the last word, so I said, "Captain Smith, do you see that man over there by the air compressor? He is the oiler on watch and it's his duty to regulate the cooling water to this lubricating oil cooler to maintain the temperature between one hundred ten and one hundred twelve degrees. If he doesn't he gets chewed out by either me or the watch engineer. So you see, I'm not any better at this temperature guessing than you are!"

He left the engine room in a huff without even saying goodbye!

The following day, I was standing on the boat deck with the chief engineer, Bill McAfee, when the vice president of operations, Captain Jones F. Devlin, walked aboard and headed for the open hatch in which the cargo oil tanks were located. McAfee remarked, "My gosh, there's old man Devlin. He was an upperclassman over me at Massachusetts Nautical School in 1924! He hazed the crap out of me then!"

"Why don't you go over there and say hello? I'm sure he'll be glad to see you," I said.

"Yeah, I think I will," and he left.

I watched as he approached Devlin, and in the next minute McAfee was holding Devlin's suit coat while Devlin climbed down into the open hatch. After his inspection in the hatch he returned, grabbed his coat from McAfee, and left the ship.

McAfee returned to where I was standing and I asked him what went on.

"I told him my name was McAfee and that when he was an upper-classman over me in school he dragged my ass all over the place. He then said, "Well, McAfee, I haven't changed a bit. Hold my coat, young man!"

I caught that right away because "Young Man" was the name given to all underclassmen in that school, and it had a derogatory implication about it! I knew that because the term was still in use when I attended the school years later!

Devlin had been aboard a few times during the conversion of the fuel deep tanks, not to check on the work, but by his presence it would be shown that he was taking his new job seriously as a senior compa-ny official. He had a few conversations with Captain Gretcher over the stability of the ship, while the oil was aboard and after the oil was discharged, and said that he should check his stability and, if neces-sary, ballast the empty tanks, but only with freshwater so as not to contaminate the internals with saltwater.

Finally Gretcher decided that while he hadn't taken a serious interest in the conversion, he had better climb into the tanks so he would be in a better position to answer any future questions from Devlin. We had just completed an internal examination of the tanks and were ready to fill them with freshwater ballast as a final test before carrying any cargo oil in them.

Gretcher had just finished conducting a safety meeting of all hands on the ship regarding the safe measures to take when entering tanks, working in them, etc. One of the points he expressly made was that no one, and he repeated, NO ONE, was to enter any tank with-out another man standing by the manhole at all times, and that every man who enters a tank was to have a safety line attached to him

After the meeting I had connected a two-and-a-half-inch fire hose from a hydrant on the pier to the ship and continued it on through the open manhole in the tank top and into the tank about five feet. I lashed the loose end of the hose to the top rung of the vertical steel ladder which left about four feet loose in the tank. By now it was lunchtime so I knocked off to eat.

In the meantime Gretcher decided lunch hour was a good time for him to enter the tank for his inspection, so he climbed down into the hatch and through the open manhole which held the hose, but without telling anyone! When I finished eating I went directly to the pier and turned on the water to the hose to begin the filling process. When I returned to the ship I was greeted by a screaming, hysterical, bleeding, soaked-to-the-skin man who hardly resembled our captain!

"Who in hell turned on that water while I was in the tank? Were they trying to drown me?" he shouted loudly.

"I did," I replied.

"Murphy, you're fired!"

"Captain, you knew we were going to start the test right after lunch, and also, why didn't you follow your own rule that no one is to enter a tank without someone standing by the manhole? And furthermore, where was your safety line?"

Gretcher had been at the been at the bottom of the tank, which was about twelve feet deep, when the water began pouring in on him, and his only escape was to climb back up the ladder, fighting the whipping of the loose end of the hose. He was constantly struck by the brass coupling as he attempted to climb by it and still hold on the rungs of the ladder while being soaked by the cold water rushing out of the hose!

While still sopping wet and trying to find someone else to blame, Devlin appeared! After hearing all the facts he chewed out Gretcher for doing such a stupid thing, particularly since Gretcher had called Devlin at the conclusion of the safety meeting to report to him that the safety meeting had gone well and that all hands were very familiar with the safety precautions to be taken! Of course, if Devlin had had his wits about him he would have chewed me out also, for not checking the interior of the tank before turning the water on, but he obviously didn't think of it!

We made a few trips carrying cargo oils to Antwerp and Rotterdam, and business was picking up with the seven sister ships on the run. The company had its salesmen wooing one oil company which shipped hundreds of tons of various oils monthly such as lubricating, tallow, tung, and fish oil to name a few, and if it could land a contract with them it would increase our revenue considerably. This particular company always shipped its cargos on product tankers, ships designed specifically for carrying liquid cargos, but we told them we had just as good service and would be cheaper.

The company finally decided to give United States Lines a try. A small tanker delivered a load of 500 tons of highly refined lubricating oil to our ship and we loaded it through hoses from their barge through the manhole covers in the tops of our tanks. Upon completion, the manhole covers were bolted down and seals applied to them to insure against tampering.

We left New York in a few days and were heading for Antwerp when our radio operator picked up an emergency call from a ship in distress just off the English Channel. The ship was called the SS *Flying Enterprise*, and was taking on water after its hull developed a crack and began listing badly. Several ships in the vicinity rushed to her assistance, including a civilian-manned United States Navy ship working for the Military Sea Transportation Service. Their captain assumed charge of the rescue operations and directed that all ships stand by to pick up the few passengers aboard and the crew when they abandoned ship. The abandoning of the ship took place without incident, but at the last minute the captain of the *Flying Enterprise*, Captain Kurt Carlsen, decided to remain on board!

Our ship was a couple of hundred miles away, but we speeded up while our captain, Jim Knowlton, fired off a message to the MSTS ship that he was steaming full speed to assist in the rescue. Almost at once we received a message from the MSTS captain: "All vessels resume your previous course; we have more than sufficient ships on scene!"

Knowlton came to my office (I had just been promoted to chief engineer on the previous trip) and told me he had a good idea which he wanted to present to the MSTS captain and which would justify our continuing steaming toward the scene. His plan was to pump our valuable cargo oil overboard to quiet the seas, much the way "storm oil" was sometimes used in the early days.

When he presented this plan to me I told him there was no way we could pump it out; the pipelines inside the tanks were blanked off plus we had no pumps with access to the tanks.

"There must be some way, chief," he said.

I told him the only access to the oil was through the manhole covers in the shaft alley (openings into the tanks for tank cleaning equipment once the cargo is discharged), but that we could not open them because they were located near the bottoms of the tanks.

The captain then said, "I have an idea. We'll slack off the bolts and let the oil dribble into the shaft alley and then you pump the shaft alley out with the bilge pump and the oil will end up overboard!"

"We can't do that. I've got boiler brick, insulation, stores, and spare parts stowed in the shaft alley."

"Then you'll have to move them, and let's get started with it," he said angrily.

I suggested he send another message to the MSTS captain and get his opinion of this plan before we went to all the work entailed in the cleaning the shaft alley, which could take all hands an entire day.

He decided to take my suggestion and sent the message. Once again he was directed to keep away from the area: "It is already too congested, and forget about the 'storm oil': it would be of no help, and also everyone is off the ship except the captain and he elected to remain, so as I directed earlier, resume your course!"

Captain Carlsen stubbornly refused to leave his ship, which was listing more by the hour, and became somewhat of a hero and was the subject of news headlines and radio broadcasts worldwide. Some commentators speculated that he was doing it for the publicity, and others romantically suggested he was following in the footsteps of Captain James Lawrence whose dying words were uttered aboard the ill-fated *Chesapeake* during the war of 1812: "Fight her till she sinks and don't give up the ship!"

Others suggested "He wanted to go down with his ship!" like so many storied captains did in pulp magazines, and still other claimed he was remaining aboard under secret company orders to "maintain a live soul on board" to prevent salvage from unscrupulous characters.

Whatever his reason, after a few days the ship developed a more severe list and he decided it was time to go so he signaled the MSTS captain that it was time he left the ship. He was picked off the vessel and the ship sank soon afterward. His rescue made headlines around the world and he was given a tickertape parade in New York on his return to the states. It had been rumored that the United States Coast Guard was planning to schedule a hearing, at which he would be required to explain why his ship got into such dire straits. Did he check the vessel's stability prior to leaving port? Was the cargo secured properly? But after seeing the reception he received from the press and the public, the coast guard backed off on any inquiry.

Perhaps if the National Transportation Safety Board had been in existence at the time, the facts leading up to the casualty would have been determined.

Meantime, our ship completed its trip to Europe and we returned to New York where Captain Knowlton told the office about his attempt to aid in the rescue and about his plan to use the cargo oil in the rescue and he received the worst verbal beating ever given in the office to a captain.

Devlin called him to his office and told him, "We've been beating the bushes for months trying to get that shipper to ship his oil with us, and when he finally decides to give us a try, you want to pump his cargo overboard! Knowlton, you're lucky that the MSTS captain told you to get your ass out of there or you'd be without a job today!"

• • •

With a fleet of more than fifty-five freighters and two passenger ships afloat on several oceans, it was inevitable that some of our fleet would come upon a ship in distress or find the need to come to the assistance of an injured person aboard a ship without medical facilities. Such was the case one time when our passenger ship the SS *United States* was eastbound in the Atlantic from New York to Southampton and received a distress call from a yacht nearby. The yacht radioed that it had an injured passenger aboard who required medical assistance as soon as possible.

The passenger ship altered its course to rendezvous with the yacht, while the engineers and mates readied one of the ship's lifeboats to make the run to the yacht. One of the engineers suggested number two boat; its engine had just been overhauled while in New York and was in good condition. Of course, strictly speaking, any boat could have been used, since all of them are always ready for operation if needed.

The passenger ship altered course to meet the yacht and, in a matter of a few hours, the passenger ship arrived at the scene where the yacht was lying. They launched the boat and started the engine as soon as the boat reached the water from the davits. Of course, starting the engine any earlier could have damaged the engine because it relies on seawater for its cooling.

A mate and an engineer plus other crewmembers rode the boat to the side of the yacht, but the engineer noted the temperature of the cooling water was steadily rising during its passage to the yacht. After arriving alongside and getting the injured man safely aboard the lifeboat, the engineer announced he had to secure the engine because it wasn't getting any cooling water and would momentarily seize if operated any longer!

Now a decision had to be made: Launch another lifeboat from the passenger ship, or tie up the lifeboat to the yacht and let the yacht tow them back to the waiting passenger ship, which in full view of a thousand passengers on board could prove extremely embarrassing!

They elected to do the latter, so the lifeboat put a line aboard the yacht and the yacht took it in tow with the injured man and several crew members aboard and slowly made its way to the side of the passenger ship. As they came alongside the passengers let out a rousing cheer, more likely for the crew of the yacht than the lifeboat crew!

The injured man was taken aboard and remained on the ship until it reached Europe. In the meantime, the engineers examined the lifeboat and discovered a new gasket in the cooling water line to the engine, installed during the engine's overhaul in New York, had been drawn up too tightly and squeezed into the opening in the cooling waterline, shutting off the water supply. To save face they called the commodore, John Anderson, to the lifeboat station to show him the cause of the engine's failure and, being the gentleman he was, he thanked them for showing it to him and told them not to let it bother them, because it wasn't bothering him—a sterling example of the type of man he was!

Of course, it wasn't recorded how many passengers thought it might be a good idea to take the yacht on board the passenger ship instead of the faulty lifeboat for the remainder of the trip, especially those passengers whose lifeboat station was boat number two!

• • •

At the time of the buildup of ships in Diego Garcia, United States Lines offered two of its Challenger I class ships, the SS *American*

Champion and SS *American Courier*, to the Military Sealift Command for charter. They were accepted, but certain alterations had to be completed prior to the chartering, such as a dehumidification system installed in the cargo holds to control the humidity, a requirement when carrying munitions, minor alterations to crew quarters, and the complete repainting of the vessels from standard company colors to stark white, except for the smoke stacks which would retain the company colors; red, white, blue.

A newly appointed assistant vice president in United States Lines was placed in overall charge of the project and I was assigned as port engineer and given the task of refurbishing the ships in Bethlehem Steel Shipyard in Hoboken, New Jersey. I wasn't sure if I would like this assignment because the assistant vice president and I had already had a couple of confrontations shortly after his appointment, not long after Malcolm MacLean had taken over the company.

After the two ships arrived at the yard, the assistant vice president called for a meeting on a regular schedule for progress reports. The meetings were usually held on Monday morning in an office on the pier and present were the various department heads from the yard as well as outside vendors assigned to the ships. At one of the Monday meetings, about midpoint in the alterations, he asked if anyone had any immediate problems with the work up to that point. No one reported any. Everything was going well and on schedule as far as I was concerned, so he asked me what my immediate concerns were at that time.

I told him I had a watertight door which was bent slightly and had to be straightened, a hydraulic hatch cover which was warped, and, I facetiously added, "a pile of garbage on the afterdeck six feet in diameter and seven feet high which I have to get rid of!" Everyone laughed at this point because it was obvious he was simply throwing his weight around at these meetings and I was giving him a zing.

"Where'd the garbage come from?" he inquired.

"From the meals served to the crew over the weekend."

"What do they normally do with the garbage?"

"At sea they throw it overboard, but here at the pier I'll have to find a way to get rid of it, but don't worry about it, it'll be gone before you know it," I said, not having a clue what I would do!

At the end of the meeting, one of the vendors, Jack Bailey, and I walked to the ship and he went to see his workmen and I went in another direction to observe the workers straightening the watertight door. About a half hour later, the assistant vice president boarded the ship to look around and spotted me.

"Show me your problems," he said.

I took him to see the watertight door being straightened in its frame and then to see the warped hatch cover.

"Well, I see you have everything in hand. Let me see that pile of garbage."

I led him through the passageway to the other side of the ship, and as we turned the corner I stood there with my mouth open! The huge pile of garbage was completely gone; only a wet spot remained on the deck!

"Well, where is it? he asked.

"I got rid of it," I replied, "I told you I would!"

"Where did you put it?"

"That doesn't matter; it's gone. That's what matters."

He headed to the rail to look overboard in the water, when I said, "Don't worry; I didn't have it thrown overboard. That's illegal!"

Probably realizing he and I didn't get along too well, he knew I wasn't about to tell him what happened to it, so he left and went back to the office.

I then went to Jack Bailey and asked him if he knew anything about it and he laughed. "Sure, when you told him at the meeting not to worry about it, I could tell you didn't know what you were going to do, so while you and he were looking at the watertight door and hatch cover I had my men shovel it into fifty-five-gallon drums and carry it to the after end of the ship and we hung the barrels over the side with brackets, out of sight."

Later that day, I called a garbage refuse truck to the pier and had it hauled away. For months later, whenever I met the assistant vice president in the office he'd say, "Okay, what happened to that garbage?" But I never told him!

• • •

The two ships were eventually accepted by MSC and, after loading in several ports, were on their way to Diego Garcia, their white hulls gleaming in the sunlight. With the exception of United States Coast Guard boats, most ships of the armed forces are traditionally painted gray, be they in the navy, army, or Military Sealift Command, for standardization and camouflage; however, white was required on these two hulls for reflective purposes to prevent their getting too hot while on station in the Indian Ocean—a seemingly dead give away that they would be carrying highly combustible materials which would require protection from too much heat!

After their arrival on station there, they were assigned routine duties such as leaving port in small convoys for exercises, or patrol or surveillance duties where they would follow a predetermined track and report any unusual findings and return to port a few days later.

Diego Garcia is surrounded by many small islands which are uninhabited, or at least are supposed to be, their inhabitants having been evacuated months earlier by the British, who controlled the islands. On one surveillance trip one of the ships saw smoke coming from the beach of one island and reported it to the British. They sent a boat to the island and removed a British citizen who had been put ashore from a yacht at his own request and reportedly "just wanted to get away from it all for awhile." He was given a one-way ticket back to England.

On another occasion, a small eruption of land was discovered peaking above the ocean in an area where charts showed no land to exist. The area was observed routinely by vessels after being reported, and gradually a small island was formed, and when considered large enough by the British, they dispatched a British officer with a flag, an oil barrel, a piece of pipe, and a bag of cement mix on one of our ships. The crew put a lifeboat over the side and transported the officer and material to the land where he mixed the cement in the barrel, shoved the section of pipe into the mix, and installed the British flag, declaring the land part of the British Empire!

A few month later this latest land claimed by the British disappeared under the Indian Ocean, never to be seen again!

Our ships remained on station for several months, performing their routines without any problems and in constant touch with the office. Weekly reports from the ships' masters and chief engineers regularly described the maintenance being carried out by the crews; thus when we received a notice from the commanding office on the island describing the deplorable conditions of our two ships, we were mystified.

The navy captain in charge strongly suggested we send a man from our office out to Diego Garcia at once to discuss the situation with him. Without any delay, my boss, Tom Young, was on his way. When he arrived on the island, he immediately got a launch out to the ships, which were at anchor in the lagoon, and began his inspection. The machinery plants were operating nicely, maintenance of deck machinery and gear was being routinely performed, and he could find no reason for the complaint.

He then reported to the navy captain aboard the flagship of the small fleet and which held the title of Commodore Ship. Tom got the impression that this phase of the captain's career in Diego Garcia was a necessary evil on his way to a more glorious command, but he had been the one who registered the complaint, so Tom would report to him.

Sitting down with him in the officers' lounge, he was told our two ships looked terrible in the lagoon in the midst of all the other gray hulls. In several areas, the white paint seemed to be deteriorating, and no maintenance was being performed on them.

Tom informed him that he was just aboard both ships and found the maintenance to be up to par and that all machinery, deck, and engine was operating and being maintained normally.

"I'm talking about the deplorable sight of those hulls," he said.

Tom informed him that the rust streaks were the result of the salt atmosphere and seawater which washed over the welds and washed away their protective coat of paint. He further reminded the captain that each ship had been issued orders from the navy that no one is permitted to work over the side of any ship while in the lagoon because of the danger of falling overboard from a staging or boatswain's chair, because the lagoon is alive with poisonous coral, sharks, and barracuda!

Tom also explained if the rust streaks were washed off, the hulls would look quite presentable, but even such routine maintenance was forbidden by their rules. Under normal circumstances the ship's crew would be overboard in boatswain's chairs in every port, wire brushing the rust and recoating the areas, and the rust would never appear.

At this point Tom remarked again that the machinery of both ships was performing nicely and that he considered the complaints to be cosmetic for the most part, when suddenly the lights of the flagship in which they were meeting went out and the ship blacked out completely! At this point Tom had to stifle a smile after just having informed him about the machinery operating so well on the merchant ships. Tom and the captain continued their conversation in the darkened lounge for several minutes, much to the embarrassment of the captain, and when he could stand it no longer, he called his executive officer.

"Call that repair ship at the next anchorage and tell them to get some engineers over here and get this plant started. We've been dead in the water long enough!"

A few minutes later, the executive officer reported to him, "Captain, the repair ship says they can't spare anyone right now; their ship is dead in the water also. All hands are trying to get their plant started, too!"

Keeping a straight face, Tom suggested that he had better go and said goodbye to the captain. He boarded his launch and returned to our two ships, brilliantly lit up with their deck lights aglow and floodlights lighting up our red, white, and blue smokestacks! The company never received any more complaints from the officials on the island after Tom's visit!

• • •

In 1971 United States Lines contracted with Sun Shipbuilding Corporation to build a group of container ships to be put into service on the company's Far East run. The last of these ships, the SS *American Apollo*, was delivered and made a couple of successful trips during its six-month guarantee period. It was on it third and last trip prior to the expiration of its guarantee when it suffered a casualty to its steering gear about 1,500 miles from the Panama Canal on its homeward-bound voyage from Japan.

A subsequent inspection revealed the carrier bearing supporting the weight of the rudder and rudderstock had failed due to lack of lubrication, caused by the lubricant retainer being installed upside down during construction. In the middle of the Pacific the crew had no way of knowing the extent of the damage and was primarily concerned with having enough rudder movement to navigate the ship to Panama. Rudder movement was limited to only three degrees to port and starboard and each movement created more wear, not to mention the resounding grinding noise it made as the ship proceeded.

The ship limped into the Panama side of the canal and the company agent, Frank Zeimetz, found an old abandoned pier to tie up the ship where a survey could be held to analyze the damage. The company sent me to Panama to conduct a damage survey and contract for repairs. In the meantime, Panama Canal authorities boarded the vessel and informed us that transiting the canal without a rudder was out of the question, even with a tugboat escort! We also found we could get no help from any shore facilities because all the available labor was fifty miles away, on the Atlantic side of the isthmus, and authorities would only allow their men to work after their day's work was completed for the canal. They could then take a train across Panama, but after a taxi ride to the pier it would be time to return on the last train back to the Atlantic side! Facing these obstacles, we decided we had to solve our problem using the ship's crew.

After removing many of the preliminary parts of the steering gear, we were able to determine the damage, and realized it was beyond the capacity of the crew to affect permanent repairs. Since no help was available, we decided to attempt to lift the rudder and rudderstock from its bearing a few thousandths of an inch by using hydraulic jacks mounted on the main deck, directly above the rudder. This would give us more rudder movement with the load removed from the bearing.

Work such as this was difficult enough to even consider on a ship tied up to a remote pier next to a jungle, but on a new ship which has little or no gear aboard, it seemed impossible. The ship did have one piece of equipment aboard which could be of use, however—a huge swivel whose weight was about 200 pounds, mounted on a bulkhead in a forward compartment. This was aboard only because it was a requirement of the American Bureau for Shipping and it purpose was for use as a spare in the event one of the two swivels holding the anchors failed. The captain dispatched the boatswain with two men to remove it from the bulkhead and bring it aft to the steering gear room. About an hour later, the boatswain, a huge hulk of a man, returned to the steering gear room crying like a baby!

"Captain, you won't believe what happened. We removed it from its mounting and were flopping it over and over on the main deck when it flopped in the opposite direction and fell through the hawse pipe and went overboard!"

The captain put his arm around the boatswain and told him not to worry; we'd figure something else to do. I admired the captain for this attitude, because we still needed the boatswain's expertise and know-how in solving our problem and he didn't want to discourage him.

The following morning a United States Army officer boarded the ship to inquire about some army cargo we were carrying, and when it would be unloaded. When he saw our plight he became very helpful. We told him we needed to locate two hydraulic jacks as soon as possible and, unbelievably, he told me they had just taken delivery of two new ones, but he was reluctant to loan them to us unless I signed for them! My signature was quite important to him and I couldn't believe we had such a stroke of luck to locate them so quickly; therefore I couldn't sign his receipt soon enough!

They delivered them and later that night we swiped an iron girder from some junk ashore, cut it into two pieces with an acetylene torch, and carried it back to the ship. We burned a hole through the afterdeck directly over the rudder, mounted the jacks on the girders, tied cable around the tiller of the rudder, and lifted the two-ton rudder one eighth of an inch, enough for us to operate the rudder twenty degrees in each direction instead of the required thirty-five.

We called a surveyor from the American Bureau of Shipping and a Panama Canal Engineer and demonstrated to them that we could control our rudder within limits and they gave us permission to proceed through the canal, providing we used a tugboat escort. Once we were on the Atlantic side we had help from a shipyard and they welded extra brackets to our jury rig to make it more seaworthy and the ship proceeded to Newport News Shipyard in Virginia where permanent repairs were made. At the guarantee survey Sun Shipbuilding was found liable for all costs connected with the casualty, including loss of the vessel's time. A check of sister ships found three other vessels with the lubricant retainer installed upside down, and these were corrected before any problems could arise.

While the ship was tied up at the Panamanian pier, our only communication with our office in New York was from our agent's office several miles from the ship. New York wanted to be kept abreast of our progress because consignees of our cargo were hounding the company for its delivery. While Captain Knowlton, Chief Engineer Ed Almberg, and I were in the agent's office waiting for our first call to New York to go through the Panamanian operator, we were having a cup of coffee and we heard a screech of brakes outside his office door. A moment later the door opened and a slinky, shapely, young lady appeared in the doorway with the sunlight behind her highlighting her silhouette and she spoke, "Good morning, Frank. Did the ship come in?"

"Yes, it's right on schedule."

Thanks, Frank," and she closed the door and we heard her drive off with a roar.

Knowlton's eyes were nearly bulging out of his head and he could hardly speak, "Wow, who's that, Frank?"

"Oh, she's a high-price prostitute, here to spend the night with the captain on the Apollo."

"THAT'S ME!" he shouted.

"No, it isn't, captain. You're on the *American Apollo*. She's here for the shrimp boat *Apollo* which just came in this morning at a pier in the cove just up the street. I call her every time the boat comes in as a favor to the captain.

Captain Knowlton slumped down into his chair saying, "I never get any breaks!"

A few minutes later, I remarked about a picture on the wall of the office which showed our SS *United States* and one of our freighters, the SS *American Challenger*, passing each other at sea. This photo had been set up by our office for use as a calendar picture a couple of years earlier and was taken from a helicopter.

Captain Knowlton remarked, "Frank, in that picture there, I was the captain on the *American Challenger* at the time the picture as taken. I just told the commodore on the *United States* by radio to hold his course and I would maneuver my ship into position for the picture and that's the result."

Knowlton appeared to be somewhat smug as he explained this, so I spoke up and said, "Yeah, Frank, and Mr. Almberg, the chief here, was the chief engineer on the *United States* at the same time. Some coincidence, huh?"

Frank said, "What? You were the chief engineer on the SS *United States*? I didn't realize that."

Frank called to his secretary, "Hey, Marie, come here. Did you realize Mr. Almberg was the chief engineer on the SS *United States*!"

"We feel honored to have you in our office, chief," Frank said.

Knowlton realized he was losing in this situation, so he spoke up and said, "Yeah, Marie, and I was the captain on that other ship at the time," but Marie was not impressed and I just sat back and enjoyed the way I set Knowlton up.

• • •

As I mentioned earlier, Captain Knowlton and I had been shipmates for several years aboard the SS *American Jurist* before I became a port engineer, and we remained good friends. The chief mate aboard the *American Jurist* was Bill Hurley at the time, and Hurley and I were always conscious of losing our hair and constantly reading up on cures for baldness. We first became aware of this when we entered the officers' dining room one evening and could detect an odor which I thought at first was fuel oil!

Hurley remarked about it and I immediately rushed outside to see if one of the engineers had spilled fuel oil on deck because the overflows were just outside the area. Finding none, I returned to sit down to eat supper and Hurley turned to Captain Knowlton and asked, "Can't you smell it?"

"No, I don't smell a thing. You must be imagining things."

Knowlton, who was sitting opposite me, attempted to change the subject, but Hurley wouldn't let up.

"Dammit, I smell fuel oil; I know that's what it is. I've cleaned up enough oil spills in my lifetime to know that smell!"

Looking at Knowlton, he noticed the captain's hair was slicked down and leaned over closer to him for another sniff and said, "That's it, you're wearing something on your scalp that stinks. That's why your hair looks so greasy!"

Knowlton threw down his fork and stormed out of the dining room, telling Hurley to mind his own business.

Later, we caught him applying an ointment which had been developed by a veterinarian to cure the mange on animals and which was manufactured from a petroleum-based product.

Knowlton had heard that it was also useful to prevent hair loss and was experimenting with it on board. When Hurley confronted him with this, Knowlton broke down and admitted it, and told us we had better consider using it also because we were both getting thin on top.

We scoffed at this suggestion, but today Hurley and I are bald and Knowlton died years later with a full head of hair, so it appears he had the last laugh.

Knowlton enjoyed reading and often attempted to take on the character he had just read about. He found a book about Horatio Hornblower, the fictional British admiral, and upon completing it began strutting about the decks, a la Hornblower, until Hurley called him on it, saying he had just finished reading about Hornblower and had put it in Knowlton's room for him to read. On another occasion, Hurley had read a book on buffalo and put it in Knowlton's room when he finished it. Knowlton, not knowing where the book came from, began telling everyone in the dining room about buffalo, their history, and background from the pioneer days. The radio operator, Jack Conroy, was in the room listening to him and asking questions when Knowlton realized Conroy had read the book and was really eggin' him on. Knowlton became aware of this and shouted, "Sparks, you bum, you read the book, didn't you? I can tell from the way you're talking. I don't want to hear another thing about buffalo in this dining room, is that clear?"

Just at that moment, Hurley entered the dining room and in a loud voice, said, "How's Buffalo Bill today, captain?"

I would rather not repeat Knowlton's reply here!

On another occasion, Captain Knowlton and I were walking down a street in Antwerp, Belgium, when he turned to me and said, "Let's cross the street and look in that store window over there."

"That's just a restaurant with the menu in the window," I said.

"Yeah, I know, but let's cross over and see what the special is today."

As we were crossing the street, a door opened from a bar opposite the restaurant and a lady stepped out onto the sidewalk and shouted, "Hey, Captain, come over here and pay your bill from last trip, you cheap Yank!"

"It sounds like she knows you," I said.

"Naw. She's got the wrong guy."

"Yeah, then how did she know you are a captain?"

Knowlton just grumbled and we continued on our way.

Many sailors learned to tell a fib to the barmaids and ladies of the evening who hung out in the waterfront bars when asked what their position was on the ship. Captains would say they were and AB and chief engineers would say they were a wiper, while conversely many ABs and wipers would tell the girls they were the captain or chief engineer! The girls would then examine their hands, and if they were not clean and well kept they knew they were being fed a line!

SMUGGLING

The United States Customs Service and our United States Coast Guard have managed to put a serious crimp in the smuggling of narcotics into this country. They have recruited ships' officers and crewmembers to be on the alert for any suspicious-looking packages brought on board the ships as well as people on the piers and along the waterfront who might observe suspicious movements.

One such case involved our container ship, the SS *American Astronaut*, which had just docked at our container pier at Howland Hook in Staten Island, New York. It was a Sunday morning and the company had arranged for cargo operations to commence at one o'clock in the afternoon, which would give the ship time to complete the formalities of clearing customs, immigration, and public health regulations.

On board was a cabin cruiser which belonged to a United States Lines vice president who had previously been in charge of our west coast operations and who had lived in the San Francisco area for several years. He had been transferred to the home office in New York and arranged to have his boat shipped to New York on the SS *American Astronaut* at this time. He and his family were now on the pier and ready to ride the boat up through New York harbor and to its new berth, a marina in the East River.

The company had made arrangements to have a container crane activated before cargo operations commenced to lift the boat from its cradle on deck and deposit it in the water beside the ship. Unknown to the vice president and his family , the ship's captain, Bill McManus, had directed the ship's chief steward to make up a picnic basket containing sandwiches, soda, and cookies to be given to the VP's family just before leaving the side of the ship for their trip.

After the boat was discharged and safely in the water, just prior to casting off its lines, McManus appeared on deck and lowered the basket to the deck of the boat and wished them a happy trip up the bay. Almost as an afterthought, McManus had also included a bottle of Scotch whiskey in the basket. The whiskey had been purchased out of bond in Hong Kong and thus had no revenue stamp on it, but McManus didn't give this a thought at the time.

Unknown to them at this time, however, a woman had been looking out her window from the New Jersey side of the Kill Van Kull just in time to see the basket being lowered to the deck of the boat. Suspecting some sort of illegal operation, she called the local police who realized they had no jurisdiction in the matter and immediately called customs and the coast guard. The boat left the side of the ship and began its leisurely trip through the bay. A coast guard boat, customs launch, and New York City police helicopter quietly began following the boat at a discreet distance, staying in touch by radio.

Soon after, a reporter from a New York newspaper picked up on the scene and started writing a story about the "chase"! After a few hours the boat arrived at the marina, and police, customs, and coast guard pounced on board. The vice president and his family were interrogated and the boat thoroughly searched, but all that was found which was illegal was the bottle of Scotch! Luckily, it had not been opened, so there was no need for any charges of operating the boat while under the influence. Perhaps if the bottle had been opened, the label would have been destroyed and no evidence would have remained that the bottle was "smuggled into the States"!

After a conference among all the participants, it was decided to forget the entire matter, including the Scotch, and the authorities left the boat. In the meantime the reporter had called in the story, up to the point where the authorities had boarded and it was now press time, so the story made the front page of the following day's edition with pictures of the chase, but without a conclusion to the story.

When the paper followed it up and realized there was no story after all, they never informed the public of the results of the chase, and people wrote letters to the editor chastising them for teasing the public abut a potential smuggling story!

On another occasion one of our ships had a slight fuel spill while tied up at the same pier in Staten Island, and the company immediately contracted with an oil spill specialist to clean it up. Their equipment included several white soft "pillows" of an absorbent material which would quickly absorb the fuel and prevent its spreading. An individual, perhaps the same person as in the previous incident, called authorities when they saw the huge pillows being gathered up by a small boat from alongside our ship.

Once again, customs, coast guard, and police converged on the scene only to find nothing illegal, but the men in the cleanup crew had a good laugh over it, much to the chagrin of the officials!

EMBARRASSING MOMENTS

It is quite easy to become embarrassed when one does not anticipate a situation which could occur while starting out on a project innocently and with every good intention.

I was sent to Rotterdam one time, accompanied by a service engineer from General Electric Company, and we were to troubleshoot a problem with the high-pressure turbine in one of our ships which was reported by the chief engineer over the ship-to-shore radio while in the mid-Atlantic. We flew into Amsterdam, took a taxi to Rotterdam, and arrived there just as the ship was tying up to the pier.

After making minor repairs and adjustments to the turbine couplings and after a dock trial alongside the pier, the repairs were completed. I called the airport for reservations to New York for the two of us and we were booked on the next day's flight. I then called the Hilton hotel in Rotterdam for reservations for the two of us for that night. There were only two rooms available—one a conventional one and the other a large salesman's room complete with sitting room, etc. Mr. General Electric took the regular room and I took the larger one.

Because the ship was sailing soon, we elected to go right to the hotel and shower there instead of aboard ship. We caught a cab and checked in and agreed to meet in either one's room after washing up and then go to supper. For this reason I left the door to my room unlocked and got out of my work clothes prior to taking a shower.

Deciding to use the toilet before showering, I was sitting on the seat and noticed a bidet mounted on the floor beside the toilet. Having seen them only in plumbing store windows prior to this, I decided to explore its operation. It had a hot and cold faucet on one end and a third type of faucet between them. I opened the right-hand faucet and a geyser of water under great pressure came rushing out of the bowl, flew upwards, struck the ceiling, and then came raining down on me! I quickly closed the faucet and sat there, momentarily stunned, soaking wet! My first thought was to wipe down the ceiling, lest the plaster softened and it, too, came plopping down on me. I grabbed a bath towel and, balancing on the rim of the bidet and reaching as high as I could, began wiping off the ceiling when I heard a voice, "Are you ready yet, George?"

It was the General Electric man and he looked in the bathroom through the open door and saw me stretched upward, naked, wiping the ceiling.

"What in the hell are you up to?"

I climbed down from my perch and told him the story and we both enjoyed a good laugh over it. He went to the lobby to wait for me, probably not wanting to witness any other stupid antics I might pull!

On the flight home, he assured me he would not mention the bidet incident to anyone, but the next time I needed a General Electric engineer, I got a laugh from their dispatcher. "Oh, yeah, you're the guy who tried to figure out the plumbing of a bidet!"

Another embarrassing moment occurred when one of our ships on the Far East run discovered two stowaways hiding in a cargo hold after leaving a port in the Orient and was homeward bound, too far from any port to return them. When the ship arrived in Oakland and San Pedro, California, to work cargo, immigration authorities were notified and inspectors boarded in each port at arrival and departure to verify they were still on board. The law required that they remain on board until the ship returned to the port where they boarded, and if they were to escape the company faced a heavy fine.

Management in our two west coast ports routinely assigned a company watchman to guard them while in the two ports without asking the master. The stowaways were locked in the ship's hospital, which was located one deck below the main deck and three decks above the engine room. The captain issued orders that the two were to be handcuffed while the ship was in port as an additional precaution against their attempting an escape.

The ship left the west coast and eventually docked at our pier in Staten Island, New York. Upon docking, the company asked the captain if he wished to have a guard assigned to them and he replied it wasn't necessary; they were handcuffed and he was certain they were quite secure in the locked hospital.

When a ship arrives at its home port, many crew members get off for vacations, new ones arrive on board, fuel is taken on board, and other stores are delivered; thus it is quite busy—so much so that the gangway watchman does not bother to check identification of men coming aboard, and could care less about the identification of those leaving the ship, especially after a busy arrival day. After this period things slack off somewhat.

The day after arrival, a Saturday, was a quiet one, with most of the crew ashore and only a handful of watch standers aboard. The mess man had delivered breakfast to the stowaways and returned a short while later to pick up the dirty dishes, but failed to notice they had managed to retain one of their breakfast utensils, a knife. In the quietness of the tween deck, and using the knife blade, they managed to remove the hinge pins from the door of the hospital, remove the door, and quietly creep around the corner to the ship's machine shop, the door to which was left open, remove a hacksaw from the tool board, and return to the hospital where they sawed the handcuffs loose.

They strolled up to the main deck, waved to the watchman who waved back, and simply walked over the gangway to the pier and to freedom!

On Monday morning the captain returned to the ship and asked how the stowaways were doing and upon discovering they were missing then realized that no one had informed any of the oncoming deck department crew that there were stowaways in the hospital! He had to report the incident to the office as well as to the Immigration and Naturalization Service that there were two unauthorized aliens loose in New York who already had a two-day start!

The company was extremely embarrassed and paid a heavy fine, and the captain took an extended leave of absence, not voluntarily!

Sometimes the most embarrassing moments occur when a person is trying to make a good impression, or is in the middle of a situation where an incident could leave the ship or company embarrassed.

A few years ago, a new regulation by the United States Coast Guard required all ships to have life rafts fitted in racks on deck in addition to the vessel's lifeboats. These rafts were encapsulated and designed to be released from their stowage if the vessel were to sink to a certain depth. The two halves of the capsule would burst open from a charge inside, and the raft would then inflate itself and float to the surface.

Just after their installation on one of our vessels, a coast guard inspector boarded to examine them and issue an approval. It was discovered that someone on board thought the breakaway holes in the bands were a flaw, and rebanded the two halves with new solid strapping he had obtained from the engine department. Needless to say, we were not issued our certificate and new strapping had to be ordered from the manufacturer.

Still another embarrassing incident occurred during a coast guard supervised lifeboat drill while our vessel was undergoing its coast guard biennial inspection.

The ship's clown (every ship seems to have one) made it a habit to carry a large, newspaper-sized knot chart folded up in his dungaree pocket to every boat drill. He knew that someday he would have a chance to use it and get a laugh from everyone. On this particular day, the captain was on the bridge supervising the lowering and raising of the lifeboats in a demonstration to the coast guard inspector of the efficiency of his crew in performing its duties.

A loose section of small rope was seen dangling from one of the boats, and in his most authoritative manner the captain bellowed, "You there, Johnson, tie off that line so no one gets hurt!"

With that, Johnson reached into his back pocket and produced the paper, unfolded it in a flourish, and said, "Yes sir, just what kind of a knot would you like, captain? I have a number of them to select from!"

The inspector turned to the captain and remarked, "Captain, I think you should know that we take these boat drills seriously in the coast guard, even if you in the merchant service do not!"

Humiliated, the captain told Johnson to report to his office after the drill, where he got a royal chewing out for embarrassing him.

Another embarrassing episode happened in New York when the coast guard boarded one of our ships and planted a smoke bomb in an area in the after end of the ship. They then reported this to the chief mate, who was busy working cargo, and told him it was an experiment with a new type of smoke producer which could not tolerate saltwater, but they wanted to observe how our crew would react when they were told saltwater could not be used. Normally, at the first sign of fire on board, the engine room is notified and the fire pump is started at once to have water pressure at the hydrants which are mounted all over the ship and ready if needed.

The coast guard fired up the bomb and disappeared from sight to observe the crew, but, unknown to them, a utility man from the galley had dumped some garbage into a container on the stern of the ship and noticed the smoke, so he threw an empty bucket overboard with a rope, filled the bucket with saltwater, and doused the bomb, ruining it! When the crew arrived the fire was out and the coast guard was livid to think their new type of bomb was now destroyed!

The chief mate then told the coast guard, "Hey, our man saw what appeared to be a fire, so he put it out as quickly as possible. We're proud of him!"

• • •

When a ship arrives in port from overseas, whether it's a port in the United States, Europe, Australia, or the Far East, each country has its own distinct methods and rules which must be met for the ship to properly "enter" that country. For instance, some nations require the crew to be checked off in the presence of an official representing that country. Another might wish to study the crew list prior to allowing crewmembers shore liberty. One reason for this is an attempt to control narcotics entering their country; known smugglers are often listed on a secret list available worldwide.

Australia is the only country I discovered, however, which required the entire crew to line up on the main deck in the presence of a doctor for a strange type of examination. With the crew in a single line, side by side, the captain and doctor would approach each crewmember, and, as the two stood in front of each man, the doctor would announce "Hands."

The crew member was to put both hands in front of him, palms up, while the doctor examined each one, and then said, "Over," and the crew member was to turn his hands so the backs were exposed. He would then move to the next position and repeat the procedure until the hands of the entire crew had been examined.

On one voyage, the ship's clown, who had been running to Australia for several voyages, stood in line as required and, when the doctor approached his position and announced "Hands," he placed one palm up and one palm down!

This action threw the doctor a curve and he said, "Just a minute, something wrong here! Over," and the clown reversed the position of his hands, still one up and one down! The doctor turned to the captain to complain, but before he could say anything the captain told the man to behave and don't make waves.

The crew member then held his hands out properly and the test proceeded, but the doctor turned to the captain and told him this was a serious test and he didn't appreciate any clowning around and furthermore he could request other tests if he so desired and delay any liberty for the crew! After this threat, everything went as scheduled!

While talking about hands giving information, I recall one time while seated at my desk in New York, the telephone rang and it was our Chinese port engineer, Tony Wong, calling from a shipyard in the Far East. He wanted to bring the office up to date on the work aboard the ship he was working on and asked to talk to our boss. I had to tell him he was out of town but I would take any message and let the boss know when he returned. The conversation went like this:

"How's the job going, Tony?"

"It's moving kind of slow, but it appears to be on schedule. I tell you what—hold out your right hand in front of you."

"Okay, now what?"

"Is your hand held out?"

"Yeah."

"Turn your palm up."

"Okay, now what?"

"Now turn your hand over so the palm is down."

"Okay, I did that. Now what?"

"Now turn the palm up."

"Okay, now what?"

"Now, turn the palm down and repeat this a few times!"

While I was turning my outstretched hand over, palm up and palm down the other port engineers in the office began watching me and scratching their heads!

Tony then said, "That's how the job is going!"

"You dumb bell, you have the entire office here laughing at me while I'm waving my hand in the air!"

I had fallen for his weird sense of humor!

• • •

The clown's antics backfired one time not long after when our ship was tied up in New Orleans and a group of us were standing on the boat deck in mid morning enjoying a cup of coffee. It was a popular place to have coffee because we could take in the sights on the pier as well as watch the cargo operations, and see who was coming aboard and leaving the ship via the gangway.

A well-dressed man came aboard and headed for the ladder leading to the boat deck. Everyone turned to see him and wondered what business he had aboard.

"Good morning, gentlemen. Is there a Matt Gauthier aboard?"

Matt (the clown) spoke up, "Yes, sir, I'm Matt Gauthier, from the great state of Connecticut. How may I help you, sir?" He spoke in a loud, proud, boasting voice.

"May I have a word with you, sir?"

"You certainly may, my friend. Please speak up. These are all my friends and anything you have to say to me may be shared by these shipmates of mine. Please speak!

The man produced a wallet from his pocket, flashed a badge to him, and announced, "Federal Bureau of Investigation!"

Needless to say, Matt was speechless. He stuttered and fumbled for words and finally blurted out, "Don't say another word. Come to my room where we can have some privacy!"

After they entered his room, he slammed the door and even locked it and, shaking like a leaf, was about to ask him what it was all about when a knock came on his door. Matt opened it and the chief mate, Bill Anderson, was standing there with a big grin on his face.

"You pulled it off good, Charlie. I've never seen Matt at a loss for words. We got you good, Matt!"

The FBI agent started to laugh and said, "I'm glad you showed up, Bill. I couldn't go on with this charade much longer without laughing!"

It turned out that Bill Anderson and the agent were longtime friends and they had set Matt up the night before over a few drinks ashore.

This incident did not humble Matt, however, and he continued his high jinks aboard as the trip wore on.

• • •

Seats in the officers' and crew dining rooms aboard ship are usually assigned so that at each meal the same seat is waiting for its assigned individual, regardless of how crowded the dining room may be at times. Often, in port, an individual may wish to have a guest for lunch of dinner, and this is easily arranged by asking a tablemate if he would mind sitting at a spare table for that meal. These requests are generally honored, because of the spirit of conviviality among the crew and officers.

Quite often the captain or chief engineer might have a guest, so the chief mate or first assistant engineer might volunteer to give up his seat. As chief engineer, I often surrendered my seat when the captain's guests were invited to eat aboard.

I was extremely embarrassed one time when, as a port engineer, I had just invited the chief dock master at Newport News Shipbuilding Company, in Virginia, to eat breakfast after dry-docking one of our large container ships. The position of dock master is probably one of the most prestigious in any shipyard and carries with it an enormous amount of responsibility, and I felt privileged he had accepted my invitation. I asked the officers' dining room waiter if it would be alright if we ate at the table usually used by the captain, chief mate, first assistant engineer, and chief engineer, because everyone except the captain had eaten breakfast already and the captain had told him he didn't want to eat breakfast because he was meeting his wife and taking her to breakfast ashore.

We sat at the table and started on what was to be a leisurely meal. We had been up since 5:30 A.M. and were both quite hungry. The waiter had just delivered our meal when the captain appeared and strode over to the table, "Who the hell is that in my seat?" he demanded.

"Hi cap. This is the chief dock master, who docked your ship this morning. I invited him to breakfast because we've been up since 5:30 this morning."

"Who in the hell gave him permission to use my seat?" he bellowed.

"I did, E.V." I said, calling him by his initials as I had always known him. "The waiter told me you weren't going to eat on board."

"I don't give a shit. Nobody uses my seat for any reason!"

I was humiliated at this point and told him we would leave his table and sit at another, but the dock master, also humiliated, said, "Never mind, George. I've lost my appetite. I'm going ashore and eat!"

"Wait up," I said. "I'm going with you!"

I later asked the captain, who up to that point had been a friend of mine, why he had behaved as he did and told him of our embarrassment, but he just shrugged it off and walked away, never offering an apology, and we hardly ever spoke after that!

• • •

And while we are on dock masters, I had just completed the work aboard one of our ships in dry-dock at Bethlehem Steel Shipyard in Hoboken, New Jersey, and the vessel was due to go into the water early the following morning. My office had called me and asked what time the ship would be leaving the dry-dock because tugboats would need to be ordered, so I attempted to reach the ship superintendent by phone to ask him. When I couldn't reach him I called the yard operations office, but no one there answered the phone. I finally called the dock master's office and was told by his secretary that he was somewhere in the shipyard, but she didn't know where.

I then called the yard telephone operator and asked her to page him on the shipyard loudspeaker system for me. My phone rang a few moments later and it was the dock master.

"Who in hell is this, paging me on the loudspeaker?"

"George Murphy, U.S. Lines port engineer. I have to know what time you plan on undocking our ship tomorrow morning so we can order tugboats!"

"Get something straight, Murphy. No one except the general manager of this shipyard pages me over the speaker system—NO ONE!"

He raged on, "If anyone needs me they can come to my office or reach me on the phone, but no one pages me. I'm the chief dock master!"

By now, I was as furious as he was and I replied, "Now you listen, Mr. Chief Dock Master, I happen to be a customer in your shipyard and I won't tolerate being treated like this. Your principals will hear from mine about this!"

He then simmered down and said, "We are flooding the dock at 0600 and you should be able to leave by 0800," and he hung up.

I told my boss about him and he made a phone call to the yard the following day and told them of the incident, but I don't know whatever became of it.

• • •

Several years ago we carried four young Catholic missionaries as passengers from the East Coast of the United States to the Philippines. When we finally arrived in Manila, they had been aboard the ship for more than a month, and by that time had fitted into the ship's routine and seemed like part of the ship's crew rather than passengers.

They left the ship upon docking and reported to their superiors in the city but returned the following day and each day thereafter to eat lunch during the five days we were in port! Our port officials then told us our ship had a change in schedule and that we were to leave Manila for Hong Kong and return directly to Manila, instead of heading for Japan directly.

We asked them if during their brief stay in Manila they had found anything they might need and couldn't get there which we could pick up for them in Hong Kong and they replied, "Yes, a good American meal. But seriously, we can't get tennis balls here in the Philippines!"

Our ship left port the following day for its trip to Hong Kong and soon returned to Manila. The young men watched the marine news for our arrival and showed up as the ship was tying up at the pier.

We had purchased eight tubes of new tennis balls in Hong Kong for them, but never thought to declare them for Philippine customs! Since each tube contained four balls, we had a total of thirty-two, but how would we get them ashore and through customs?

The missionaries, who were dressed in their white tropical robes, told us not to worry; they had plenty of deep pockets in their outfits. In the privacy of my office, we opened the packages and they began distributing the balls in their robes. They each managed to conceal eight of them, but they did look lumpy!

We watched from the ship as they approached the customs gate in the pier area. The customs officials, being Catholics like the majority of the population there, began bowing to them, and in a grand manner the missionaries raised their right hands in a blessing gesture, and out popped two tennis balls. They bounced in the direction of the customs officials, and while the missionaries attempted to retrieve them, more fell out, and then the customs began chasing the balls as more and more fell to the ground, bouncing all over the gate area!

Everyone, missionaries and customs, had a good laugh over the situation, and no one questioned them about where the balls had come from.

• • •

United States Lines operated many ships during World War II under the Bareboat Charter to the War Shipping Administration. Most were freighters, but we did operate a few passenger ships which were used to carry American troops to Europe. One of these ships, motor ship *John Erickson*, had just left the east coast and was hardly at sea when a colonel in charge of the troops realized there was not enough activity aboard to keep several hundred men busy and occupied.

After all, they could only do so much calisthenics daily, it was too crowded to jog, not everyone wanted to join in a poker game, and, although morale was high, these guys knew what would probably be the biggest and most frightening adventure of their lives lay just ahead in a matter of a couple of weeks. The colonel consulted with the captain to see if he had any ideas to keep his men occupied, and the captain told him to give him a little while; he'd try to think of something.

Later, while taking a shower, the idea hit him. He had just unwrapped a new cake of Cashmere Bouquet face soap and noticed a coupon on the wrapper. A little later, he confronted the colonel. "I got an idea, colonel. I'll have my men deliver several thousand cakes of face soap to your men on deck and in the holds and you can have your men cut the coupons from all the soap wrappers. We have thousands of cakes of soap and packages of soap powder on board and each has a coupon. When we get them all cut out, we'll send them to the soap company and get some premiums from their catalogue!"

"What good will that do our troops? They'll be in Europe when the prizes arrive on board."

"Yeah, but at least they'll have something to do to take their minds off the war for the time being!"

The colonel agreed, and the crew and GIs spent the next couple of days bringing soap up from the storerooms to the decks and holds. The GIs began cutting when someone suddenly realized they couldn't throw the wrappers overboard. After all, nazi subs made it a routine to surface and study the surrounding water to look for traces of garbage, refuse, etc. in attempts to track ships.

The wrappers were saved for disposal ashore, while the hundreds of thousands of coupons were boxed up and ready for shipment to the manufacturer when the ship returned to the States. The captain had mailed a letter from Europe to the Octagon Soap Company in the States requesting a catalogue be mailed to our company office in care of Captain Kenneth Sutherland, United States Lines.

When the ship returned to New York, the catalogue was delivered, and Sutherland realized he had enough coupons to get at least one of everything in the catalogue, so he sent them off requesting everything! He received a reply which stated, "Please note, each wrapper contains a message which reads, 'Valid only when redeemed by the final purchaser.'"

He had to concede the final purchaser in this case was not his ship, but the GIs and crewmembers who used the soap, but he felt some consolation knowing he had given the GIs something to do to take their minds off the war.

My friend Tony Wong, many years before he became a port engineer, was serving aboard the ship as a plumber, and was called to a large compartment in which were berthed several army officers. They had complained of a leaking toilet in their quarters and Tony was dispatched by the chief engineer to repair it. Tony had been on watch at night in the engine room when called so he picked up some tools and quietly entered the compartment so as not to awaken any of the officers. After quietly repairing the toilet, he noticed several drinking glasses containing partial dental plates and dentures belonging to the officers and each placed in a secure area so as not to tip over. He quietly exchanged locations of several of the glasses and swapped dentures in others in what he thought would be a humorous gesture!

How humorous it turned out to be he never found out, but did learn that pandemonium broke out in the morning when each man attempted to put his teeth back in his mouth! This he heard from an engineer who had gone into breakfast and the officers were discussing it with the captain!

• • •

All of our new ships were fitted out with air conditioning while under construction. This had been a sore spot for the company in earlier ships which relied on wall fans and blowers for ventilation. The unions began a crusade to encourage the company to modify the existing ventilation systems in these earlier ships to include air conditioning, but often the modifications were a feeble attempt to pacify the crew.

Also, individual room air conditioners were purchased and installed in the windows and portholes of crewmembers' rooms on another class of ship, but these weren't too satisfactory either.

The central air conditioning system installed on our new Lancer-class ships proved to be very effective and not only added to the comfort of the crew, but in a sense was acclaimed as a minor victory for the unions, because during the early planning stages of the ships it was not considered.

One of the main reasons the company didn't want the systems was because they feared too many people would attempt to control the temperature in the midship house. It would be impossible to satisfy forty-three people at the same time! As an example, one captain was constantly attempting to adjust the temperature in his quarters by adjusting his thermostat by using the thermometer reading on the thermostat. After a lesson by the chief engineer, who explained that the thermometer had no bearing on the setting and was merely the temperature in the room, the captain was satisfied and learned to live with the system. The captain's explanation was, "It didn't work that way on the passenger ship I was on!"

Aboard the SS *American Lynx*, one of the Lancers, someone didn't think the air conditioning system was cooling the midship house quickly enough and adjusted the basic system controls in the engine room, thereby causing the air conditioning chiller to freeze and rupture the entire bank of tubes. The internal leakage of the cooler introduced water into the compressors, and this demolished the internals of the compressors so no one had any air conditioning for the balance of the voyage.

Because the union contracts of the officers and crew stated if the air conditioning system was inoperative for longer than any twenty-four hour period they were to be paid lodging for each day of the voyage, an amount which would be staggering for the company at the end of the trip, which still had seven weeks to go. The engineers stripped the compressors down and sent back a massive list of spare parts needed for repairs and the company made an all-out effort to supply them by flying them to various ports in the Far East.

It was an almost futile effort because a shipment would arrive in an airport in Taiwan only hours before the ship was due to leave the country and the shipment would be delayed by the local customs! When finally cleared and released, the ship had left the country and the parts were forwarded to Hong Kong, a free port which didn't care so much about customs, but delayed the shipment in order to examine the contents of the boxes to be sure it wasn't contraband!

This comedy of errors repeated itself several times in the various Far East ports because the spare parts were being sent piecemeal as they became available in the States!

The ship finally arrived in New York with the air conditioning still not functioning, but after reviewing the circumstances concerning the damage and the all-out effort made by the company to get the spare parts to the ship, the unions decided to forgive the company and not hold it to the requirements of the union contract. Of course, no one was sure just who the individual was who made the damaging adjustments to the system, and each union was well aware it could have been one of their own. The company had the system rebuilt while the ship was in New York.

However, while the ship was in New York, the captain asked if I would have the refrigeration repair company furnish a room air conditioner for his bedroom.

"I have the dimensions of the room on this piece of paper, and don't worry, I'll pay for it myself; the company doesn't have to know about it," he said, handing the dimensions to me.

He then said, "You know this central system failed last trip and I am a big man and I perspire profusely, so I should have my bedroom cool!"

This put me on the spot. He obviously didn't have a clue about the ramifications of such an installation.

"I can't do that, captain. Every man on the ship will want one if you get it and the entire ship will have air conditioners hanging out every window!"

"I don't care about the rest of the crew; I'm only interested in staying cool. The rest of the men are not as large as I am!"

I told him, "I'm sorry, captain, but unless you get an okay from the office, I'm not permitted to do it."

A few hours later I had a call from my boss.

"George, go ahead and get the air conditioner for the old man. His boss gave the go-ahead, but tell him he has to pay for it!"

I told the supervisor of the repair crew to measure the room to verify the dimensions and deliver a new air conditioner to the ship in care of the captain, and that the captain would pay for it. I then informed the captain of the decision made by the office and he would need to have a check ready to pay for it upon delivery.

A new Carrier air conditioner was delivered the following day, and the ship left port a few hours after it was delivered. After clearing the port, the captain opened the box and removed it and, after analyzing the shape of the unit and comparing it to the size and shape of his bedroom window, he realized he had quite a project ahead of him. He called the chief mate and the chief engineer and, after a careful survey of the situation, a plan was developed for the installation.

It would require altering the shape of the window because the conditioner was wide and the window narrow, thus it became necessary remove the internal paneling from the room, remove the insulation, burn away a section of the external steel bulkhead, trim the removed steel, and reweld it in place to suit the outside dimensions of the unit!

When the unit was finally installed, the engineers informed the chief engineer that this was the same as new construction and their union contract stated they should be reimbursed at the overtime rate for any installation normally performed by a shipyard!

Needless to say, the captain blew his top upon hearing this, but could do little about it except to agree to pay them for it out of his own pocket! The installation was completed just after the vessel cleared the Panama Canal and headed for Long Beach, California, and it was in constant use after that until they reached port. Upon docking in Long Beach, the captain asked our port captain, Everett Bell, to call a Carrier serviceman because it wasn't cooling satisfactorily. Everett asked who would pay for it and the captain told him it wouldn't be necessary because it was under guarantee.

The serviceman showed up, examined the unit, and exclaimed, "I can't touch this machine, it's built by Canadian Carrier. It'll have to go back to the factory as far as I'm concerned!"

He left the ship and, after the ship left port, Everett Bell received an invoice from the serviceman for $70.00. He asked New York what to do with the invoice and was told to hold it until the ship returned to Long Beach after its Far East trip and present it to the captain!

The ship returned in about six weeks and Everett presented the bill to the captain and he blew his top, again!

"I'm not paying it; it's under guarantee!"

Two weeks later, the ship arrived in New York and as the ship's port engineer, I met it upon docking. The chief engineer reported that the repaired central air conditioning was operating normally and that he had installed a lock box around the controls to prevent any more tampering. He then informed me about the engineers requesting overtime for the installation of the captain's air conditioner, but during the voyage home, they held a meeting and decided they would not ask the captain for reimbursement. Apparently they had second thoughts about it because, after all, they had to live with him and it really wouldn't be fair to do this to a shipmate.

In the meantime, the captain asked me to have the supplier of the air conditioner remove it from his room and take it ashore to their shop and check it out—"It didn't seem to be putting out!" as he put it. I told him I would call the company who furnished it, but he would have to remove it for them. This produced more grumbling, but he had the mate remove it and I called the company to pick it up.

A few hours before sailing for the next trip he asked me when the company planned on returning the unit and I told him they were not repairing it, but were crating it up for shipment to the factory in Canada.

"What? You mean I won't have it for this trip?"

"No, I thought you knew that. They won't touch it if it's under guarantee!"

"Tell them to bring it back then; it isn't that bad. I can live with it the way it was!"

By now I was at my wits end, but I called the supplier and told them to return it as is and leave it in the captain's room.

When they returned the unit, I accompanied the men to the captain's room and told them to dump it in the middle of his deck and leave it there!

The captain grumbled and said, "I've never been so frustrated in my life, and all over a lousy air conditioner!"

I said, "Captain, you have no idea what frustration is yet. Here's the bill from the Carrier serviceman in Long Beach. Everett Bell mailed it to me on orders from the company and they expect you to pay it" and I left the ship!

I learned later that he sent a personal check to pay the bill!

COMEDY OF ERRORS

I was supervising repairs aboard one of our vessels in a shipyard in San Francisco several years ago and one of the repair items was to renew the gasket on the side port. A side port is a door built into the hull of the ship at the tween deck level and is used for taking stores into the ship. The storerooms and walk-in refrigerators are usually located on the tween deck, thus the door offers easy loading to these compartments.

The door is constructed so that it fits flush with the hull, with internal hinges so as not to have any protrusions on the outside which could be broken off or struck when docking. The crew had reported the door leaking slightly at sea; thus the repair. The vessel had completed its dry-docking and was now secured at a wet berth in the shipyard to finish up loose ends. The yard had elected to make the gasket repair while at the wet berth rather than in dry-dock to save constructing a high scaffolding from the floor of the dry-dock up to the door.

The crew opened the door from inside the ship using the hydraulic pump installed for that purpose so that the door was now swung out over the pier. An enterprising shipyard worker assigned to the repair elected to erect his own type of scaffold from the ground to the height of the door, about ten feet, by moving a steel refuse bin into place under the opened door and placing wooden planks on its top. This made a handy platform at just the right height.

I left the yard at this point to have lunch with the yard superintendent, the first time I had left the yard for lunch since the ship arrived several days earlier. We returned from lunch just in time to see the side-port door resting on the platform and the worker laboring away removing the old gasket, unaware that the door was moments away from being damaged. We hadn't planned on the tide going out when we left for lunch, and now the entire ship was about to be resting on the refuse bin! I shouted to a nearby burner who was using an acetylene torch to hurry over to the ship and burn away the side of the steel refuse bin to give the side-port door clearance as the tide continued going out.

At this point, the door was just touching the steel bin and barely resting on it, so we couldn't pull the bin free. The burner began burning away the steel when suddenly the contents of the bin, a pile of wood, began burning furiously. Another worker, seeing the flames, rushed to a nearby shipyard fire hydrant, unrolled the hose, and carried it to the fire. He signaled to another worker to turn the water on and, while doing this, the crane operator, high up in the air in his gondola, and oblivious to the goings on below him, started to move his crane along the tracks, severing the fire house which was laid out across the tracks!

In the meantime, the burner continued to burn away the steel amidst the heavy smoke, but the loose end of the hose attached to the hydrant was now out of control and began to flail wildly, and spraying saltwater all over the crane wheels and driving machinery and eventually into the drive motor, which emitted a bright flash. The crane stopped abruptly as the motor burned out!

The burner had successfully burned away enough of the steel bin to give the door clearance; thus the ship had no damage and the bin was then pulled away from the ship's side and the fire put out using hand extinguishers.

The vessel left the yard on schedule the following day and I remained in the area for another two days to settle the bill for the drydocking. During the negotiations, the shipyard estimator asked if we were planning to pay for repairs to the electric motor and a new fire hose and I told him we were not. I reminded him that when the ship entered his yard, we signed a contract, the first page of which contains a "red letter clause" which states "The yard shall not be responsible for consequential damage suffered to the vessel as a result of faulty material or workmanship," and is usually printed in red.

I told him that same clause applied in the other direction equally; that the ship owner is not responsible for consequential damage suffered by the yard from work performed aboard the vessel by the yard. I was bluffing, but it sounded pretty good and the yard accepted it. Of course, the yard realized it should have constructed a safe platform under the door for their man to work from and one which could easily have been moved when they realized the tide was going out.

Also, I am almost certain the cost of the motor repair and a new hose was buried somewhere in the invoice I signed!

The red-letter clause I mentioned is found on all shipyard and repair yard contracts, and must be agreed to before any work can be carried out. As it was explained to me one time, a ridiculous example would be if a shipyard installed a leaking rivet in the bottom of the hull of a ship and the ship sank as a result, the yard's liability was merely to furnish a new rivet! The loss of the ship would be considered consequential!

I was sent to the west coast another time to give a deposition in a lawyer's office about a particular manufacturer's boiler failures. United States Lines had a few ships whose boilers were manufactured by this company and we were one of several companies called to give depositions.

After giving the deposition in the lawyer's office, he took me to lunch. Over lunch he remarked how glad he was to get some work from United States Lines, and he hoped he would be used by them for any west coast legal work in the future, because we had no legal representation there.

I had mentioned the red letter clause and he smiled and said that reminded him of one job he had where a new west coast shipyard had just opened and the owners asked him to compose a red letter clause for them for use with future work in the yard. He told me he read a few others and, using these as a guideline, worked one up for these people, but he had left a loophole in the wording just in case he might need to use it at some future time! He then added, "And guess what? The opportunity came a couple of years later when I was representing a client against that yard and I was able to win the case for him because of the loop hole!"

Needless to say, I lost all respect for him at that time, and when I returned to our office in New York I informed my superiors of our conversation and his name was quickly removed from our list of prospective lawyers in that area.

CAPTAINS

In 1984, when the company contracted to build twelve diesel driven Econ-class ships in a Korean shipyard, a decision was made at that time to utilize bridge control for operating the diesel engines. Prior to this, bridge control had been attempted only once before in the company, on its Lancer-class ships which were driven by steam turbines. At that time labor problems arose between the Marine Engineers Beneficial Association and management when the MEBA maintained the deck officers were performing the work normally done by engineers, such as maneuvering the engines. These complaints were eventually settled; however, the company elected to continue using the engineers for maneuvering when a series of mishaps occurred while using bridge control.

In one instance, aboard the SS *American Legion*, a new third mate was on the bridge just prior to sailing and was told by the captain to open the throttle only enough to spin the turbines alternately ahead and astern to keep the turbines warm just prior to leaving port. He told the captain he had been on another bridge-controlled ship and he was accustomed to that practice. The bridge console held a circular dial which was calibrated form 0 to 100 and which indicated percentage of throttle opening when in use. The mate opened the ahead throttle and the ship surged ahead quickly, breaking its mooring lines and then ramming into the stern of the vessel ahead, causing damage to both vessels.

A damage survey was held and the third mate insisted he had operated the throttle correctly and that there had to be a malfunction in the automation in the engine room. Technicians were called in and nothing irregular could be found with the automation, neither on the bridge nor in the engine room. Needless to say, the departure of both

84

vessels was delayed while repairs were preformed and underwriters paid the claim for damages to each vessel citing machinery failure.

Several years later, while talking to some people in the office about the new ships' automation, the captain remarked, "I hope they school everybody in its proper operation. I recall on my ship one time, when the third mate opened the throttle too far and we rammed the ship ahead. He thought the dial on the console indicated revolutions per minute, but its purpose was to show percentage of throttle opening, and the kid didn't know that!"

I shook my head for a moment and then took the captain aside and asked why he hadn't told us that at the time. I explained our insurance claim would have been much simpler because we were insured against "crew negligence," and we could have saved the considerable expense of having the automation checked out at the time, not to mention the vessel's delay. He flushed for a moment, realizing I was the port engineer who was handling the ship then, and told me the third mate was a friend of his and he didn't want to get him in trouble!

In another instance, one of our Lancer-class ships was approaching the pilot boat to pick up the harbor pilot and, instead of reducing vessel speed gradually, the captain attempted to make a crash stop in the vicinity of the pilot boat by suddenly closing the ahead throttle and opening the astern throttle to brake the vessel's forward motion. Unknown to him, however, the engine room machinery went into fail-safe mode when the throttle was suddenly closed. The level of the water in the two boilers dropped momentarily, as is normal, but this sent a signal to shut off the fires and close the throttle to the turbines, tripping them out. Now, no amount of turning the hand throttle on the bridge would exert any influence on the engines!

In the meantime, the vessel, out of control, got caught in the trough of swells and began rolling heavily. The second mate and a couple of crewmen had just cranked open the side port to await the pilot boat's arrival alongside when they took a big green sea aboard through the open door. They managed to close the door against the vessel's rolling, but the passageway was now flooded and the seawater began pouring down onto the automated console in the engine room, flooding it. Meanwhile, engineers were desperately attempting to reset the controls, relight the fires in the boilers, and reset the trips, while others were spreading polyfilm over the console to prevent its shorting and grounding out from the cascading salt water!

The plant was restored, the vessel managed to pick up the pilot, and the ship proceeded into port. After docking, the chief engineer went to speak to the captain about the crash stop to tell him of the problems involved and he denied attempting that kind of stop. The automated typewriter in the console, however, had recorded the entire episode, logging the exact times of throttle closing, boilers shutting down, and throttle tripping out. When confronted with this the captain just shrugged his shoulders and walked off!

With knowledge of these horror stories in bridge control it was decided to set up a two-day seminar in the company's classroom to teach the captains the proper operation of the diesel engines in the new ships. Instructors were to be manufacturer's representatives and the class would run on a Monday and Tuesday. The company reserved several rooms at a local motel near the office and instructed the captains to report on Sunday and to be ready for school the following morning. About forty captains showed up, many with their wives, and checked into the motel. I knew all of them, having worked with them aboard ship or in the shipyard, and many of them had started work with the company the same year I did.

On Monday morning they appeared on the scene and I had a chance to renew some old acquaintances at that time. They told me they were having a cocktail party that evening in the lounge of their motel and invited me to attend to have a drink.

I accepted and left the office at 5:00 P.M. and walked to the motel where I saw all of them assembled in the lounge, with their wives, and all talking at the same time! They didn't see me because I had stayed out of sight behind the entrance. They had much to talk about. Some hadn't seen each other for years and others had memories to recall, still others talked about their experiences aboard our passenger ships, but these words were carefully chosen because wives were present!

I approached their waitress when she left the lounge and told her who these men were and she seemed quite impressed, and I hinted she could anticipate a healthy tip from them. I explained to her that many hadn't seen each other for a long time and that's why everyone seemed to be talking at once, trying to outdo the other with sea stories. I then asked her to go to the doorway of the lounge and, in a loud voice to interrupt their conversations, shout out, "Captain" and see what happens!

She carried it off well. All at once the loud din of chatter ceased and each captain swung around in his chair and, almost in unison, replied loudly, "Yes?" And then I made my appearance in the doorway.

They knew they had been had and half of them shouted, "George Murphy, you bastard. You put her up to that!" I strolled in with a big grin, saying, "Good evening captains. How about that drink you promised me?"

CLONES OR MIMICS

When a new third mate or third assistant engineer reports aboard a vessel for the first time, he must make himself acquainted with the personnel he will be working with as well as his routine duties and responsibilities. These he will learn from his superiors and should spend his extra hours observing the routines and customs already established in his department. On deck the captain might wish to school him on certain wording to be used when he writes up the deck logbook, the procedure to be followed when relieving the watch, his duties while the vessel is working cargo on his watch in port, and so forth.

In the engine room the chief engineer would have similar requirements for watch standing, logbook entries, and work assignments while in port. The company manual outlines these procedures and routines in a general manner; however, they leave the details to the captain and chief engineer.

Some of these details can leave a lasting impression on a young officer as he continues in his career, raising his license and gaining increasing responsibilities, as he earns promotions and changes ships in the fleet. When he reaches the position of chief mate or first assistant engineer he suddenly realizes his next promotion will be one of decision making, procedure planning, and reporting to the office instead of to a higher authority aboard ship. It is during this period in his career when he will begin to more closely observe the workings, characteristics, and little foibles of his superior and decide which of these he would most want to adopt for himself to keep the vessel operating smoothly. Similarly, it is his chance to decide to accept or reject any of these traits with which he doesn't agree.

One such example in the engineering department is the chief engineer filling out the noon report which shows the fuel consumed per twenty-four-hour-day, as well as fuel consumed per mile. If his ship is one of a class of eight in the fleet, for example, he watches this consumption carefully so that his ship will average about fourth or fifth in the group when the company compares the eight ships for operating efficiency. The best in the class will be suspect if that ship consumes too few barrels in comparison, and the worst will have some explaining to do to management why its consumption is so high! This "rearranging" of fuel numbers is easily accomplished by declaring the vessel's consumption in port to be higher than it actually is. For some reason the office never seemed to be interested in port consumption; thus a few barrels gained on paper in port each day can be consumed on paper while at sea, when the consumption calculation counts! This is a lesson in "sleeve fuel" one learns as he eyes a chief engineer's position.

On deck, the captain will have his own routines for correcting and storing charts, navigation procedures, watch-standing requirements, etc. On a lighter side, the chief mate or first assistant engineer can pick up small idiosyncrasies of his superior and carry them through to his first ship as master or chief. I was serving as a relief chief engineer on one ship and had known the captain for years when we came up together as thirds. One of the good practices he had picked up was the routine of a weekly ship inspection. I always favored these inspections because they gave us an opportunity to discover small problems before they became big ones. The inspection team was made up of the captain, chief engineer, chief mate, chief steward, and purser. The areas inspected were the public spaces in the ship, such as the galley, laundry, toilets, passageways, officers' and crew's dining rooms, and lounges. Crew and officers' staterooms were not inspected out of respect for privacy, nor was the bridge or engine room inspected. The inspection gave the crew an opportunity to point out any faulty radiators, minor water leaks in sinks and showers, dirt accumulations, rusting areas, etc. The faults would then be corrected by the ship's crew.

As we began our first inspection I saw that the captain wore his officer's hat with the scrambled eggs, though he never wore it at other times, and he mentioned something about "so the crew will know I'm the captain," though they surely must have known who the captain was on a ship with a crew of only thirty-nine men, but I said nothing. As the inspection progressed, I noticed he had a distinct type of strut as he led the inspection party. His left hand was placed on his hip in such a manner that his elbow was thrust slightly forward and he seemed overly erect as we proceeded through the compartments. This was not his normal stature and I quietly dismissed it as we carried on. We held inspections weekly, and at the next one the procedure was the same—the hat and strut. He and I had gone ashore several times in various ports to eat dinner and he never strutted at those times, but only during inspections. During many of our conversations we had discussed people in the company we knew and had sailed with and he kept bringing up the name of a captain I'll call Captain Jones.

"Did you ever sail with Captain Jones, chief?"

"No I don't know him, I've heard of him, but never met the man," I said.

"He's a fine man, good shipmaster, great captain."

As we talked from time to time I heard more and more about Captain Jones.

Our ship had now arrived in Brisbane, our last port in Australia, when our agent informed us a sister ship was due to arrive later that day from the States and would tie up just forward of our ship. It's master was Captain Jones.

Our captain came to my office and, with a big smile said, "Hey, chief, Captain Jones' ship is due in today and it's tying up just forward of us, so now you'll finally have a chance to meet him!"

I tried to act thrilled, but I don't think my acting was very good, because the captain just shrugged his shoulders and left when I appeared to seem indifferent to his announcement. Later that day, I was standing in the captain's office looking out his forward porthole when I saw a man walking down the pier toward our ship. He carried himself very erect, shoulders back, left hand on his hip, with his elbow thrust forward and strutting!

I turned to our captain and said, "Captain Jones is coming down the pier toward us." The captain rushed toward the porthole and, looking over my shoulder exclaimed excitedly, "Yes, that's him!"

A moment later he said, "Hey, you said you never met him. How did you know it was Captain Jones?"

"Oh, I guess it was just my instinct," I replied.

• • •

Whenever a new ship enters a port for the first time the company will notify the port authorities in advance of its arrival in order to gain publicity for the company, and maybe take out an ad in the local paper to encourage local shippers to be aware of the vessel's speed and characteristics and invite them aboard for an open house. This is all done to gain a little edge on the competition in the shipping industry. There are similar celebrations when a company opens a new facility in a port, such as new piers, office buildings, or cargo handling capabilities.

One of our ships became the first to enter the newly renovated container handling pier in Hong Kong several years ago, and during the welcoming ceremonies the mayor of the city presented an engraved silver tray mounted in a mahogany frame to the ship. The engraving read, To the Captain, Officers and Crew, SS American Lancer, upon being the first United States Lines ship at the newly renovated container terminal in Hong Kong. The ship's regular captain was on vacation at this time, and the captain on board was the vessel's regular chief mate and he accepted on behalf of the company.

When the ship returned to the west coast on its homeward-bound voyage, I happened to be on the west coast working on another ship as a port engineer, but paid a courtesy call aboard the *American Lancer*. This was usually done by port engineers in a port where no port engineers were stationed to see if there was any way he could assist the vessel during its short stay in port. I had spoken to the chief engineer and then went to the captain's office to visit. He had the plaque on his desk in his office, and while I was reading the inscription he remarked, "Pretty nice, huh?"

"Yeah, it's beautiful," I said, "it'll look nice on that wall right there," pointing to an empty space next to where several similar awards were mounted.

"Like hell. That goes home with me at the end of this trip!"

"You can't take that with you. It was presented to the company and the ship; not to you personally!"

"I don't care; it says to the captain."

"And officers and crew also. It was meant to be displayed on board."

"Well, I'm still taking it home at the end of this trip."

I left the ship in disgust and the vessel left port shortly after for New York. Two weeks later I was at our terminal in Staten Island, NYC when the same ship arrived. Once again I boarded the ship and found two captains in the captain's office—the regular captain who had just come aboard, back from vacation, and the chief mate who had been captain the previous trip.

Seeing an opportunity for a little kidding, I walked over to the wall where I had suggested the plaque be mounted, rubbed my hand over the area, and remarked about is emptiness.

"What are you talking about, George?" the regular captain asked.

"That new silver plaque which was presented to the ship in Hong Kong last month to commemorate the ship's first arrival at the new container terminal!" I blurted out.

"Well, mate, where is it?"

"It's in the bedroom, captain."

"Let's see it," and the mate led him, with me following, into the adjoining bedroom where his suitcase was lying on the bed.

The mate opened it and there lay the plaque in its mahogany frame, nicely wrapped in a towel.

"You can't take that home, mate. It doesn't belong to you!"

I grinned at this until I heard the captain continue, "It's mine, I'm taking it home, I'm the regular captain on this ship. You're not!"

"What the hell are you talking about? It doesn't belong to you either. It belongs to the ship and the company. I don't believe this!" I said.

The captain had previously prepared a Bloody Mary for me, but I walked out of their office and told them to keep the drink. I was too disgusted with both of them to enjoy it!

The following day I again boarded the ship. The mate had since left for home, and I was pleased to find the captain busily mounting the plaque on the wall. "I had second thoughts about it, George. Besides, I have enough of them at home already," he said, trying to get a rise out of me.

"I'll have that Bloody Mary now," I said.

"George, let me show you what my wife does with my money in Florida while I'm out at sea," and he produced a photograph of a pink Jaguar sports car. I was admiring the car when he handed another picture to me, a front view of the same car, but he quickly grabbed it from my hand and attempted to conceal it when I grabbed it back for another look.

"I don't believe this," I said, after studying the picture for a moment.

In Florida a front license plate is not used, but the Jaguar has a split center area in the front bumper to hold a plate and in this area on his car was a plate which read Captain. He knew what I was referring to and said, "Aw, it's something my wife insisted on; I had it installed for her."

"Yeah, I'll bet!"

I finished my Bloody Mary, wished him a good trip, and left his ship shaking my head!

That particular ship was one of a few in the fleet where the permanent captain did not think the vessel's chief mate was worthy of the higher position, and the same situation existed on some ships in the engineering department as well. Both captains and chief engineers soon changed their attitudes about this when told by management that if they didn't like being relieved by their subordinates, they would not have a relief for their vacation. After this ultimatum, the chief mate and first assistant engineer were gladly welcomed as their reliefs!

• • •

Many years ago one of our ships, the SS *Pioneer Gem*, was tied up in Tahiti overnight, working cargo. This was routine for these ships which were on runs from the east coast of the United States to Australia. After being at sea for about ten days out of Panama, an overnight at the island was a welcome relief for the crew. Of course, it was always a foregone conclusion that the ship would have to spend the night there for cargo operations because the captain and chief engineer would gradually slow the vessel down during this run from Panama. Cargo operations would usually only require about four hours working time, but the city of Papeete, Tahiti's only port, did not have any lights in its short navigation channel from the sea buoy to the pier so its transit could only be made in daylight. Conveniently, the ship would arrive just at sundown and thus be "stuck in port for the night." This was no surprise to the company, which seemed to accept the extra time in this port as a matter of routine. The vessel would always be scheduled to sail at dawn, as soon as the channel was visible, and of course the crew was expected to be aboard at that time. To insure that no crew members remained ashore at sailing time, the department heads counted their men at least one hour prior to leaving. As a further assurance that no one remained behind, the chief of police would board the ship and personally interview the captain to be sure.

On this particular morning several of us were gathered in the officers' dining room prior to leaving while the chief was talking to the captain over a cup of coffee.

The captain said to the chief mate, "Mr. Mate, are all your men aboard?"

"No, I'm missing two men." The chief of police made a note of their names.

The captain then asked me, "Chief, are all your men here?"

"No, I'm missing two men also," and I gave the policeman their names.

To the chief steward he asked the same and he replied he had three men missing. At that point the third assistant engineer, Reuben Tyner, who had just returned aboard from a night of drinking, turned to the captain and asked, "Captain, are all your men here? You're asking the department heads and you're the head of the deck department!"

"Mr. Tyner, I'm the captain. I'm the head of all the departments!"

"The head of any department should be about to perform the job of anyone in his department, captain. Can you go into the engine room and oil the engines?"

"Mr. Tyner!"

And before he could say another word, Tyner blurted out, "And can you cook?"

The captain stared at him with a wild look in his eyes and he shouted, "Mr. Tyner, you are heading for the logbook," and he then looked at me for approval.

I just stood there and told Tyner to be quiet and go to his room and get some sleep.

The captain appeared to be peeved at me for Tyner's outburst, but I told him I had no control over what a drunk might say. But Tyner knew that if he wasn't ready to turn to at 0800 the old man would log him for failure to start his workday, so he was up and working on time that morning. I told him to stop making waves in our department and that all of us had to live together and we didn't need problems like he created.

Tyner's attitude merely proved what he had told me when he came aboard at the start of the trip. He was the only man in the company who worked his way up to chief engineer and then got demoted, rank by rank, back down to third assistant engineer!

In the meantime, the missing crew members showed up and we sailed on time.

• • •

When a ship enters a foreign port customs officers will board the vessel to lock the ship's tobacco and liquor in a locker and apply a seal to the lock. This is because the liquor and cigarettes are usually purchased tax free and only allowed to be consumed at sea. Cigarettes are a valuable commodity in most ports and a handsome profit can be realized on the black market if they are accessible to the crew. This procedure is carried out on freighters and passenger ships; however, on passenger ships this requirement also includes locking up the bars and cocktail lounges.

On one occasion, while the SS *United States* was docked in Le Havre, France, customs allowed the bars to remain open because the ship was to be in port for only a matter of a few hours while some passengers departed and others boarded. The captain, John Tucker, was standing in the foyer near the cabin-class bar observing the passengers when the kennel keeper approached him and said, "Captain, how about letting me buy you a drink? We've been shipmates for a few years."

The captain replied, "Yeah, okay, Jim, but I'll buy."

"No, let me buy, captain. I make more money than you do!"

"What!"

"Yes, sir. Sit down and I'll tell you about it."

"Go ahead; I'm all ears," Tucker replied.

"Well, we can carry a total of fifty animals in the kennels on the top deck. The passengers were not allowed to visit their pets while in the kennels, company rule, so they have to rely on me to clean their cages, brush them, water them, and feed them. Their owners must rely on me to take care of them, so their tips can go as high as twenty bucks per passage of seven days. "Fifty times twenty comes to a thousand bucks, captain, and that's only one direction; the same people will be returning sometime in the near future, so that's like money in the bank.

"Four seven-day trips a month comes to four thousand a month, and that's not even considering my pay and overtime for each trip. Of course, the kennels are not always full, but then it just seems that when we carry a fewer number of pets, the passengers tip a little heavier, so things even out!"

At this point the captain was shaking his head and said, "Yeah, you can pay for the drinks. I'd have a double Scotch on you, except that I have be sober when I take this big ship out of port, so I'll have to settle for a soda!"

Later, thinking about it, the captain finally realized why the kennel keeper never took a vacation!

When I discussed this with Captain Tucker, he laughed and told me he thought I was about to question him about the time aboard the ship when a socialite was New York-bound from Europe and taking her prize poodle to the States to enter her in a series of dog shows. She had turned her award-winning animal over to the kennel keeper when she boarded the ship in England with strict orders for the proper care of the canine. She had proved to be extremely frustrated during the passage because she was denied permission to visit the dog and sharply criticized company policy excluding visits to the kennels by pet owners!

She followed proper procedures for landing the dog after docking in New York, quarantining the dog as required by regulations, and then removing her from custody. Soon after, while observing the dog, she noticed its strange behavior and took the dog to the vet.

The vet, believing he had good news for the woman, smiled and declared, "Congratulations, your dog is pregnant!"

Needless to say, the woman was livid. Now she claimed the dog was ruined for future breeding, and she alleged the dog had been "violated" while in the care of the United States Lines. She wrote a nasty letter to the company, threatening to sue, and vowed never to travel on a United States Lines ship again.

The letter was handed to Captain John Green, marine superintendent. When the *United States* returned to New York from its next European voyage, he called Tucker to his office and handed the letter to him, saying, "Here, Tucker, take care of this!"

Captain Tucker opened it, read it, and, half smiling, remarked, "Hell, I didn't have anything to do with it!"

"Neither did I," said Green. "At least you were there; I wasn't."

They had a good laugh over it, knowing there was probably no way the woman could prove her mutt was impregnated on board, and eventually the matter was dropped.

• • •

And while we are on dog stories, Reed Clark and I were dispatched to the Far East to interview various shipyards for their potential use in dry-docking our Military Sealift Command ships which were stationed in the Far East. Reed was in charge of this fleet and our mission took us to the city of Koahsiung in Taiwan where we were to stay for two days surveying facilities. One evening we took a taxi to the center of the city to have a leisurely supper and decided to stroll back to the hotel via a side street, somewhat off the heavily traveled highway.

We were walking slowly, observing the neighborhood sights, when Reed spotted two dogs having sex in the gutter several feet away.

"Hey, George, look over there at those dogs. Let's move in for a closer look!"

"Are you crazy? Leave them alone. You wouldn't want someone to watch you, would you?"

"Oh, come on. I'm going closer."

With that, he moved nearer the dogs when suddenly the male dog left his female companion, rushed toward Reed, bit him on the leg, then quickly returned to the female to resume his "work"!

"That SOB bit me!" Reed screamed.

"I'm not surprised," I said. "I told you not to bother them!"

I examined his lower leg and found the dog had sunk his teeth into the calf of Reed's leg through his trousers, and the wound was beginning to bleed.

We rushed back to our hotel where we washed the wound and wrapped a makeshift bandage around the leg. We began to discuss rabies and many other horrible possibilities, none of which made him feel any more comfortable!

We were leaving Taiwan the following day for San Francisco, so he decided to wait until he returned to the States before seeking treatment. Upon our arrive in San Francisco he visited his father, who was a doctor, and he took over the treatment.

Reed never did tell me what story he gave his father about the bite, but I'll bet it wasn't the truth, or his father would have probably told him he couldn't understand how a son of his could be do dumb! At least that's what I would have told my kids!

THE CREW

The crew on a merchant ship is made up of several ratings, many requiring particular skills, such as boatswain, engine utility, able-bodied seamen, engine utility man, oiler, fireman, electrician, etc. Others, however, are unskilled and need only seaman's documents certifying they have passed a lifeboatman's test, food handler's test, or lookout's test.

One of these unskilled men is a wiper, an individual, whose duties include painting in the engine room, wiping up oil spills, and general all-around cleaning of the engine spaces. Sometimes a man who had been an oiler or fireman previously would accept a wiper's job just to have work without any responsibility.

My ship was about to leave on a trip from New York to Australia, a trip which would normally take from four to six months, depending on which ports would be added to the schedule as the trip wore on. We left New York, called at various east coast ports, then Gulf coast ports, through the Panama Canal, to Long Beach and San Francisco, California, and then across the Pacific Ocean to China, then to Australia, back across the Pacific to the northern coast of South America, to Halifax, Boston, and finally New York. On such a trip we would normally screen each crew member carefully during the coast-wise section of the voyage to give us chance to get rid of any dead-wood before departing on such an extended trip. There is nothing worse than being stuck with a man who does not pull his weight on such a long voyage.

Such was the case with a wiper I had in the engine department. We had picked him up in one of the Gulf coast ports and then head-ed for the Panama Canal. He was seventy-five years old, wore thick glasses, and, unknown to me, was partially deaf. He had all the required documents to work aboard the ship, so I had no valid reason not to accept him.

Upon leaving Panama for Long Beach, California, my problems began. The day-working crew in the engine department complained to me that he was knocking off work at 11:30 each morning instead of noon, rushing to the crew dining room, eating lunch quickly, and then taking a noon-hour nap in his bunk. I made it a point to be in the engine room the following day to observe his behavior. At 11:30 A.M. I could faintly hear the dinner bell being rung in the main deck passageway by the cook. The wiper suddenly seemed to come to life, put down his cleaning rag, and headed out of the engine room for the mess room.

I stopped him and lectured him about working until 12:00 noon each day as per his union contract. He was very apologetic and I left the area. A moment later, I returned to find him heading out of the engine room. I followed him and he went directly to the dining room. I lectured him again about his working hours and finally realized he had not heard a word I had said. The following day he left the area again at 11:30! I came to the conclusion that although he was hard of hearing, the pitch or decibels of the dinner bell seemed to get through to him, and he knew when he heard that bell it was time to eat!

I finally did get through to him but could see he would be a hazard in the engine room, so I limited his work to shining handrails, a task I thought would be harmless. I told him to simply shine the rails and anything else that needed polishing. It is important to keep the handrails clean and dry because crew members enter the engine room at the main deck level and sometimes slide down the rails on their hands, often skipping several steps at a time when going below.

A few days later I received an emergency call from the third assistant engineer on watch in mid afternoon; "Hey, chief, the feed pump in use just threw all its packing from one end of the pump. I secured it and started the other one and everything is okay, but I can't find anything wrong with the pump I secured!"

I raced below because the main feed pump is one of the most critical pumps in the operation of the steam plant. When I examined the shut-down pump, the packing glands appeared to be normal and everything seemed okay. I looked away for a moment and noticed the old wiper standing with his hands on his hips and with a bewildered look on his face.

"Aren't you supposed to cleaning the rails," I asked.

"I lost my rag, chief!"

"What do you mean, you lost your rag?"

"I had a rag in my hand and I was just starting to polish that shiny shaft and the rag just disappeared!"

That solved our problem. The shaft he attempted to shine was the pump shaft which was rotating at 3,000 revolutions per minute. It seized his rag in an instant and if he had kept a tighter grip on it, it would have drawn his hand and possibly his arm into the pump and caused severe injury!

I discussed the problem with the captain and we arranged to have the man resign and flown home from our next port.

RADIO OFFICER (OPERATORS)

The radio operator, as he was called for many years, was a department of one and worked a staggered eight-hour day. He was on watch from 8:00 A.M. to noon and then again from 3:00 until 5:00 P.M. and again from 7:00 to 9:00 P.M. while the ship was at sea, but in port he had no hours! He was usually one of the first people ashore after the vessel docked, having secured his "plant" by pushing three or four buttons and turning a couple of switches!

At sailing time his start-up was usually the same procedure, but in reverse. In those days messages were sent and received in Morse code, so "Sparx" had a secure job because usually no one else knew the code unless one could remember it from his Boy Scout days!

Aboard the SS *American Jurist*, the third assistant engineer, Harold Slater, asked the radio operator to teach him the basics of operating the radio while the ship was en route to Europe. In the meantime he studied Morse code, and after a few lessons he knew enough about the job that Sparx let him send the ship's arrival message approaching New York!

The RCA operator in New York who received it remarked, "Sparx, you're a little slow on the key today!" but the regular operator took over and explained that he was just a little hung over!

A few years later, single side band radio came on the scene and voice was then used, and it was obvious that the radio operator's job was soon to be eliminated. Not long after single side band was in use, satellites began orbiting the earth and the radio operator was history. During those years when the operator was used, their union pressured the companies and the United States Coast Guard to change their title to radio officer. This was only proper because of the technical qualifications they were required to have.

One radio officer, Gene Kauder, with whom I sailed, told me he had been on a ship where the captain's wife was making the trip. The trip was nearly over, the Christmas holidays were just ahead, and the crew was wondering if the company would bring the ship to the pier before Christmas or have it adjust speed to dock after the holiday, a practice often carried out to eliminate longshoremen holiday overtime.

He received the message via Morse code that the ship was to "Make all possible speed, safe conditions permitting, to dock in time for Christmas." He typed the message onto a company radio form and rushed to the captain's office to give it to him. He knocked on his office door, but his wife answered and told Sparx the captain was taking a shower, but that she would give him the message as soon as he finished. He handed it to her, she read it, and then said, "Sparx, if you promise not to tell anyone, I'll let you read it, but you must promise; you know how he likes to be the one to pass this kind of news on to the crew!" He stood there, dumbfounded at what he had just heard, and rather than explain to her that he had to know what it contained because he had just typed it, said, "No, never mind. I'll just wait until he tells everyone," and he left the room shaking his head!

CADETS

In June of 1961, after eighteen years of going to sea, I was asked by the superintendent engineer, Joe Cragin, if I would like to end my seagoing days and accept a job in his office as a port engineer. I consulted with my wife and she told me in no uncertain terms that I had better accept the offer! She had been raising our kids, attending schoolteacher conferences, acting as family chauffeur, and doing all those things a father would normally be doing while his children were growing up. It would mean selling our house in Massachusetts and moving to the New York area where I would become a commuter, but we agreed it would be worthwhile.

During my first few weeks in the office I discovered many perks, such as an assigned contractor for each day of the week to take the port engineers to lunch; an expense account; mileage for using my car going to the various piers where our ships tied up; and invites to many marine industry dinner dances which were held almost monthly by various organizations such as the Hague Post of the American Legion; an annual dinner dance held by the American Legion post within United States Lines, consisting of employees only; the Chiselers; Marine Square Club; and the Society of Marine Port Engineers to mention a few.

Another perk was the presenting of the United States Lines Leadership Award to a deserving cadet at each of the maritime academies: Fort Schuyler, Massachusetts, Maine, and Kings Point. A graduate from each school was usually asked to make the presentation, so I, being the only port engineer from Massachusetts Maritime Academy, was selected for that one.

The first time I was to make the presentation, the governor of Massachusetts, a man by the name of Endicott Peabody, was on the platform with many other dignitaries. When it became my turn to make my presentation, I realized the recipient of our award was also named Peabody, but no relation to the governor, so after the cadet and I were introduced to the assemblage, I walked over to the governor and announced, "Because this cadet bears the same name as your distinguished governor, I believe the cadet would much rather receive his award from the governor than from me."

I then handed the box to governor Peabody and asked him to do the honors. He had just finished his speech and was now seated comfortably in his chair, relaxed, when I caught him off guard! He mumbled something to me which I couldn't understand, but I told him to simply read the nameplate on the box. He then stood up and, reading the nameplate, handed the box to the cadet. They shook hands and, in the meantime, I had already taken my seat. At the end of the graduation ceremonies, I apologized to the governor for catching him off guard, but he shrugged it off, explaining to me, "Hey, this is an election year. I need all the exposure I can get!" and we both laughed.

Obviously that extra exposure I gave him didn't help him because he lost his reelection bid the following November!

I also learned that our granting of an award at each maritime academy served another purpose—we were to become recruiters for newly licensed third assistant engineers and third mates and were expected to address the cadets and attempt to convince them that we were the company for them to join.

This recruiting effort was not exclusively ours, but we were joined by representatives from many steamship companies all with the same purpose. Each of us was armed with a batch of job applications and handed them out freely to the new graduates. One port engineer, Joe Farr, was the principal officer of the Brotherhood of Marine Officers, a union set up in American Export Lines, and he was also on the Board of Visitors of Maine Maritime Academy. He convinced that school to graduate their senior class one month earlier than the others, thus giving American Export Lines first choice of the new grads.

Ironically, when Joe retired I was appointed in his place on the board, and now had mixed emotions about recruiting. Where would my loyalty be? With the Maine or Massachusetts graduates? The problem solved itself after three years because I had to resign from the board because I was out of the country too often and could not attend their quarterly board meetings.

On one occasion at Massachusetts Maritime Academy I addressed a group of graduates just prior to graduation and told them of the trade routes the company had, the number of ships we operated, chances of promotion, and answered any questions regarding employment in the company. Upon completion of my talk another company's representative was given the same opportunity and he was followed by another, so each class could weigh all the factors in choosing their new job.

When graduation was over, I noticed a young female cadet graduate who had not been in the group I had addressed earlier, standing with her parents and apparently a boyfriend. Expecting that she knew me as a United States Lines representative, I approached her and asked, "My dear, do you have any plans after graduation today?"

She looked me squarely in the eye and said, "Sir, I plan on going right home!"

Needless to say, I didn't expect such a reply, and blurted out that I was sorry and left the area quickly; especially after the look I got from the boyfriend! She later apologized after talking to some of her classmates who told her who I was.

Today, I still present an award to a deserving cadet, but am now representing the Society of Marine Port Engineers of New York at the graduations. Due to the scarcity of jobs today, if I were ever to hand out employment applications at these ceremonies, I would be swept off my feet by the onrush of cadets and would end up flattened by the swarm.

• • •

For many years United States Lines was operated under an Operational Differential Subsidy from the government, and because of this the company had to employ cadets from the United States Merchant Marine Academy for their year to be spent at sea. These young men and women looked forward to this year at sea because it gave them a chance to be away from their regimen of studies as well as the rigid discipline they were under at the academy, plus the company paid them a small salary which was quite welcome.

It was understood that the officers, especially the captain and chief engineer, would assist them in their practical training as well as their on-board studies which were to be completed and submitted to the academy at the end of each trip. Most ships' officers welcomed them on board; however, a few thought them to be just so much ballast and tolerated them.

Most often cadets were assigned in pairs, one deck and one engine, to each ship, but on occasion only one might be assigned, depending on their availability. This occurred on one of our ships and the captain was irritated because the cadet assigned was in the engine department. This captain was not one with whom the engineers got along too well, either. It was obvious from the outset of the voyage that the captain was annoyed at only one cadet.

The ship was on a trip to the Far East and was to be gone for at least three months. So the cadet thought it would be novel to raise a beard for the first time in his life. The engineers encouraged him, knowing the captain didn't appreciate bearded officers, especially in the dining room, although none of them sported one.

After a couple of weeks' growth, the captain hinted to the cadet that he likes to see "his" cadets clean and nicely groomed, but didn't directly order him to remove his beginner's beard. When the ship reached its first foreign port the cadet went ashore and was swept off his feet by a "young lady of the evening" who picked him up in a local bar. About a week later, he began to show the effects of what he suspected were the early signs of a venereal disease, so he quietly went to the purser who, in addition to his clerical duties, was a trained medical technician and the ship's medical officer.

The purser gave him a massive injection of penicillin, being guided by information from *The Ship's Medicine Chest At Sea*, a medical book usually found aboard each American merchant ship. The purser entered the treatment in the medical log, as required by law, but said nothing to anyone. A few days later the captain was reviewing the medical log, and upon finding the entry for the cadet questioned the purser about it. The purser told him he didn't think it was necessary for him to know about something as personal as this, and the captain went into a rage.

The captain then told the cadet once again to shave his beard. "But, captain, this is the first time I've ever had a chance to grow a beard and I just wanted to see what I would look like with it. That's why I'm doing it."

"Don't argue with me, young man. I said shave, and if you refuse, I'll enter it into your fitness report to the academy and write a letter to your folks to tell them you had to be treated for venereal disease!"

The cadet was shocked to hear this threat, so he rushed right to his room and shaved. He told the ship's engineers about the threat and they were so furious they made a pact to stop shaving for the balance of the voyage, which still had two months to go. Then, in a grand display of camaraderie, at the next fire and boat drill each engineer threw his razor overboard while the captain stood on the bridge wing doing a slow burn.

When they arrived in New York at the end of the voyage, the cadet reported to the outpatient department of the marine hospital where he was examined and found to be free of any disease. I boarded the vessel as the ship's port engineer and was overwhelmed at the scruffy appearance of all the engineers, each of whom could hardly wait to shave, but had made their point!

I had sailed with the captain during my seagoing days and was well aware of his cranky attitude, and he and I never hit it off very well, so I could understand the attitude of the engineers. When the vessel had left New York on its voyage, I had asked the chief engineer, Dick Lenox, to pick up a couple of bottles of Kikkoman soy sauce while in Japan. Favors such as this were always done for each other, and the chief, a former shipmate, was glad to do it for me. He mentioned that he was glad I had asked him because he wanted to get a couple of bottles for his wife also.

When ashore in Yokohama, he stopped in a store where he was known from previous shopping trips, purchased four one-half gallon jugs of soy sauce, and had it delivered to the ship that evening while he continued on to a restaurant ashore. The delivery man left it in care of the gangway watchman, a company employee and old reliable friend of the chief engineer.

The chief returned to the ship at about 9:00 P.M. that night and was greeted by an angry watchman. He told the chief the captain had returned to the ship about a half hour before and, looking around the area near the gangway, saw the bottles. When the watchman told him the bottles belonged to the chief engineer, he picked them up and threw them overboard, saying, "We don't allow liquor about U.S. Lines ships!"

When the watchman told him it was soy sauce, the captain remarked, "Well, it's too late now. How was I suppose to know?"

Needless to say, the chief was livid and immediately thought, *This is his revenge for the cadet.*

He went at once to the captain's room, awakened him, told him off, and also told him two of the bottles were for George Murphy, the port engineer.

I later remarked to the chief that he probably felt a little more satisfaction at that point to think he killed two birds with one stone! I had hoped to say something to him about the soy sauce the next time I saw him; however, shortly after, while on vacation, he was killed in a plane crash while taking flying lessons.

• • •

A few years earlier this captain had been assigned to one of our Mariner-class vessels, which were new to the company. The Mariners had been built by the government to upgrade the American flag merchant fleet and were expected to be grabbed up by several companies; however, the cost was felt to be too prohibitive at that time. Each was operated by American flag companies for the government for a guarantee period and then laid up in the maritime commission lay-up fleet where their value depreciated at regular intervals.

When their value reached a particular point, several companies took advantage of the cheaper price and all of them were grabbed up quickly. United States Lines took eight of them and they were towed out of the lay-up fleets and reactivated in various shipyards around the country.

The ship to which this captain was assigned was towed from the James River lay-up fleet to Newport News Shipyard where it was to undergo its reactivation. Its previous captain, who was aboard during its guarantee period, had constructed a plywood bulkhead with a door across the passageway leading to his office and stateroom. This gave him complete isolation from the passageway, and thus the rest of the ship, but blocked a door leading to the outside on the boat deck.

When our captain discovered this he remarked, "This is great. With this 'wall,' I'll have my own private entrance to my quarters from out on deck as well as the passageway."

The port engineer, Nick Bachko, was supervising the reactivation and he walked up to the plywood bulkhead with the captain and, in front of the chief engineer, me, and others, marked a big X on it, saying, "This goes. It's wood, it's illegal, and it blocks the exit door to the outside from this deck."

The chief engineer let out a big laugh, which of course, was not appreciated by the captain. The captain was furious, but knew he didn't have any argument; however, from that point on we suspect his attitude toward engineers was formed!

If he had given it serious thought, he would have realized that the bulkhead was a fire hazard and blocked the escape from the living quarters and would never have passed the inspection required for upgrading the vessel's safety certificates.

• • •

The Far East run of United States Lines was one which was very popular with many crew members and officers because of its many enjoyable ports of call, one of which was Honolulu. The usual stay could be up to five days, depending upon the amount of inbound, export, and military cargo carried. For this reason a Far East ship was also often sought after by the cadets from the Merchant Marine Academy for part of their year to be spent at sea as required in their curriculum.

The engineering cadet assigned to my ship, the SS *Pioneer Ming*, on one particular trip was a fine young man who had proven to be intelligent and eager to learn. While his education aboard ship was partly my responsibility, I would also be indirectly responsible for his behavior because I would be completing his fitness report at the end of the voyage and the young man was aware of this.

So I was somewhat taken aback when he approached me while tied up in Honolulu. The ship had docked on Friday and was not due to leave until the following Tuesday and he was off duty from Friday night until Monday morning. On Saturday morning at about 9:00 A.M. he came to my office and said, "Chief, I would like permission to spend the night ashore this evening and also permission to take one of the blankets from my bunk ashore."

"What!"

"Yes, sir. I met a young lady last night from Oregon in a soda shop at Waikiki Beach. She's a schoolteacher here on vacation, sir, and we thought it would be pretty neat to sleep on the sand on Waikiki tonight, sir."

Of course this request caught me off guard; however, my first thought was "Lucky guy!" But I couldn't show this emotion to him; after all, I was indirectly responsible for his behavior.

"This is highly irregular, cadet," I said.

"Yes, sir, I realize that, sir. That's why I'm asking permission, sir."

When I regained my composure, I said, "Well, I guess it'll be okay. You're a big boy and can take care of yourself."

I filled out a property pass to enable him to take the blanket through the gate by showing the pass to the company guard.

He thanked me and left my office, pass in hand, and was only a few steps away when I called to him, "Cadet!"

"Yes, sir," he said, rushing back to my office.

"Don't forget to shake the sand out of the blanket before you come aboard, and report to me when you return."

With a big grin, he replied, "Yes, sir!

When he returned the following morning he reported to me that he was aboard, I asked if he had had a good time and, blushing, blurted, "Yes, sir!"

"Did you shake the sand out?"

"Yes, sir!" he replied with a huge grin!

For the remainder of the voyage that lad would do anything for me. I've often thought about him in my retirement, wondering if he recalls that pleasant weekend as perhaps one of the highlights of his young life, and maybe even what a good guy that chief engineer was.

• • •

I recall one time while attending a meeting of the Society of Marine Port Engineers in New York I was approached by a woman who asked if I were George Murphy. I replied that I was, and I asked if I could help her.

"I certainly hope so. I understand you are a graduate of Massachusetts Maritime Academy. Is that correct?"

"Yes," I replied.

"And also you are on the Board of Visitors at Maine Maritime Academy. Is that correct?"

"Yes."

"Then I must assume you know people at both schools. Is that correct?"

"Yes, so far everything you have asked is correct," I said.

She continued, "Well, it's imperative that our son gets admitted to either one or the other when he graduates from high school next month. He has already submitted his application. Can you help us in this regard?"

"Well, I don't know your son, but I certainly know his father, who is a good friend of mine, and based on that friendship I'll be glad to recommend him for their consideration."

And then something occurred to me that was puzzling, so I asked, "His father is a graduate of the Merchant Marine Academy at Kings Point. Why doesn't he apply for entrance there?"

And then came the put-down: "Heavens, he could never pass the test to get into that school!"

After choking back any choice words for her, I told her I would see what I could do for him.

I called the admittance officer at Maine Maritime Academy the following day and asked about her son's application and was informed the boy had been accepted that morning and his parents were about to be notified. I then called the woman and told her the good news, but added that he did it on his own and I didn't have a thing to do with it!

GUN CREWS

The Liberty ship to which I was assigned after graduation from Massachusetts Maritime Academy in 1943 had an armed guard on board made up of several gunners, a couple of gunners' mates, and an ensign as the armed guard officer. They were a good bunch of young men no older than I was. Most were right out of high school, rushed through gunnery school, and put aboard my ship and hundreds of other Libertys which were being delivered from various shipyards throughout the country at periodic intervals.

These young men were filled with patriotism and, after a short period of testing the mettle of the ship's crew and claiming squatters' right over the merchant crew because they had made one convoy trip to Europe and most of the merchant crew were new on board, everyone settled down and got along nicely.

At sea early one morning one of them came into the engine room where I was on watch and asked me to cut a piece of copper tubing from a roll of tubing hanging on the bulkhead in the ship's machine shop. I asked why he wanted it and he told me he needed it to repair a damaged piece of tubing on one of the hydraulic systems of their gun controls. Not giving it a second thought, I cut a piece about fifteen feet and he thanked me for it.

About two weeks later, while on watch, I discovered five one-gallon jugs lined up in a remote area of the engine room. They contained a liquid which resembled nothing that would be found in an engine room, at least from my brief experience. I noticed most had a cork loosely fitted in the neck, but one had a screw cap. I said nothing to anyone, but observed them each day, and soon noticed a foamy goo oozing from beneath each cork.

I finally asked the first assistant engineer if he knew anything about them, and he told me the gun crew had made a still using an old fire extinguisher and some copper tubing—copper tubing I had given them to repair their guns! Knowing their gunnery officer would not have approved of a still, they sought the cooperation of the first assistant engineer, whom they knew could do justice to a bottle of liquor.

His part in their plan was to provide a hiding place for the jugs, and for his cooperation he was to receive one of the jugs when the fermentation and aging were completed.

A few days later our ship took part in the Normandy Invasion, and while at Utah Beach, with bombs dropping, gunners firing at German planes, and all hell breaking loose, I heard a loud explosion. Believing it to be the result of a bombing run from a German plane, which were frequent at the time because we could hear everything going on up above through the engine room ventilators, my oiler, fireman, and I ran for cover under the generator flat for protection.

And then we smelled it—a sweet, sickening smell—and I shouted to my watch mates, "It must be that poison gas the British had schooled us on during one of our briefing sessions prior to the invasion!" Not having any gas masks in the engine room, we ran for the rag box to grab pieces of cloth to hold over our noses and mouths during the gas attack.

After what seemed ages, we removed the rags from our faces and left the area, and then I noticed pieces of fruit and other garbage clinging to the bulkheads in the area along with several pieces of broken glass. Our frightening explosion had been the jug with the screw cap. The fermentation process had built up a pressure and, with the screw cap, had no escape!

I called the first assistant and told him about it and he and the gun crew came below and removed the remaining jugs and threw them overboard. We later learned from the army that several GIs had been poisoned from drinking homemade liquor.

Prior to the invasion, the gun crew was constantly drilling, cleaning, and maintaining their guns, as well as drilling the merchant crew on their operation because the merchant guys were the substitute gunners in an emergency. To relieve the boredom, one of the gunners had his hair cut by the crew "barber" in the shape of a large V in honor of Winston Churchill's famous two-finger salute for victory. Other members of the gun crew put their heads together, literally, and without telling the gunnery officer, had their hair also cut with other letters so when they stood together their hair spelled VICTORY. One additional gunner wanted to get in on the act, so he had an exclamation mark cut into his hair.

They then assembled on the main deck in the proper order and another gunner brought their officer to the boat deck where he could look down on his men and read VICTORY!

He was upset at first, but then realized it was a good way to ease their tension and complimented them on it. He made one stipulation, however, that when they went on shore leave together they were to walk single file and always sit down in a manner that the word VIC-TORY! would always be properly spelled out!

Not long after a British newspaper published a picture and story about our gunners and their "victory!"

• • •

United States Coast Guard
Marine Inspection Office

The written examination for a marine engineer's license is a lengthy one, usually consisting of about seventy-five questions. The questions cover steam and diesel engineering, electricity, refrigeration, mathematics, United States Coast Guard Rules and Regulations, and safety, and are increasingly more difficult as one progresses from third assistant engineer to chief engineer.

Today these examinations are multiple choice and upon completion could be graded several miles away in a central clearinghouse, but years ago the exams were held in a large room which held from thirty to forty individuals. Usually at least two United States Coast Guard officers, one each for deck and engineering licenses, monitored the room and were there to clarify any questions regarding the content or meaning in the exam as well as to grade the exam papers as they were completed and submitted to them.

The examination usually lasted from three to five days, depending on how much one wanted to include in his answers because some of the questions were essay type and others included drawings. The routine was for the inspector to select one of perhaps five different exams, each of which contained fifteen cards, each one holding five questions each, and assign that exam to the individual. The man would then take the top card to his seat and answer its questions, return the card and answers to the inspector, and then take another card and repeat the routine until all the cards had been answered. The man could leave the room anytime after turning in a card and answer sheet and either go to the bathroom or outside for a smoke or even go home for the day.

Most individuals would take a break after each card and perhaps go outside to review notes for future questions or just relax. One morning I went to the men's room after completing a card and met a fellow there who was also taking a test and he asked me if I had gotten any electricity questions yet. I happened to look under the short bulkhead of one of the toilets and saw the seat was occupied, so I quietly told the fellow not to discuss anything there because we weren't sure who was in the stall, suspecting it could be an inspector.

The following day we met again in the men's room and the same seat was again occupied, so I quietly stood on the toilet bowl in the next stall to look over the wall and discovered a pair of navy blue pants draped under the seat and a pair of shoes under them. We never found out who thought up this scheme, but we reported it to the inspectors and they sent a sailor into the head to remove them, without comment!

While taking my examination for chief engineer in Boston, there were about twenty men taking tests. Our desks faced the front of the room where four inspectors were seated at desks facing us. Two of them were lieutenant commanders, one a chief petty officer, and the other a warrant officer. We were settled into our first cards for the day when one of the lieutenant commanders began chatting with the other, having little to do because none of us had yet submitted our first card for grading.

"Boy, that was some party we had last night," one said, yawning and stretching.

"Yeah, I'm still partly hung over myself."

The chief petty officer added, "Yeah, me too, but I learned one thing there—how to light a cigar quickly," he said, taking a cigar from his desk drawer and squirting lighter fluid on its end.

In the meantime, the warrant officer told one of the lieutenant commanders to turn sideways and he would sketch his profile on his yellow pad.

The chief petty officer reached into his desk drawer and removed a cigarette lighter and lit the end of the cigar while it was in his mouth and it flared up. Unknown to all four officers, just at this time the door behind them opened and an admiral strolled in to observe the examination room. We heard the door open and could see the entire scene unfold in front of us as the admiral let out a loud "AHEM!"

The warrant turned and, spotting the admiral shouted, "Attention!" All four stood up at once, the "artist" dropping his yellow pad, the chief extinguishing his cigar, and the yawner attempting to compose himself! We were witness to this fiasco, but were under no obligation to stand. We were merely exam takers, but had we had an opportunity to warn them of the admiral's presence we could have breezed through our exams. As it turned out, all of us completed the card we were working on and left for the day. None of us wanted to confront them after that episode.

• • •

On one occasion one fellow sitting for his first assistant engineer's license asked me how I would answer a question he had just answered on turbo-electric drive on a ship. When he repeated the question I had to admit I didn't know the answer because I had never sailed aboard that type of vessel, so he wondered if he would get it correct. Later that day, one of the inspectors called him to his desk and asked where he had found such an answer because it didn't agree with the answer the coast guard had on their answer sheet, but at the same time it seemed to be a logical solution to the problem presented in the question. He told the inspector that particular problem showed up on a ship on which he had served one time and his answer was the way the chief engineer solved it.

The inspector told him he would take his answer under advisement and not mark his paper at that time. The following day he announced to the man that he had been given full credit for his answer and that it was added to the coast guard answer sheet as another solution to the problem. Had he been answering a multiple choice question he would have failed the question.

One other time I had to make a drawing of a water tube boiler, and upon completion of the drawing in pencil it had to be inked in. After inking over the pencil image, I realized I had forgotten to include a peephole in the firebox, so I attempted to erase an area and rubbed a hole through the paper. (A peephole is purposely built into the casing of a boiler to allow examination of the quality of flame while underway). I drew an arrow to the hole and labeled it "peephole." When it arrived on the inspector's desk I saw him hold the paper up to his eye and look through the hole and then he called me to his desk.

"Mr. Murphy, you didn't have to go to this extreme to make a peephole," and turning the paper over on its other side where I had drawn the side view of a fire tube boiler he said, "and is this supposed to be a peephole in the combustion chamber of the boiler?"

"No, sir, the hole only applies to the water tube boiler!"

"Okay, we'll accept it as is," he said, and I got full credit for both drawings.

On another question I had to make a drawing of a tail shaft where it penetrated the hull for mounting the propeller, and I left the packing gland out of the drawing. He called me to his desk again and wanted to know if I intended to be a design engineer or an operating engineer. When I told him an operator, he said, "Good thing, because a ship with this installation would sink about an hour after it got into the water!" and I got only half credit for that drawing.

These are examples of the intimacy test takers could have with the inspectors who we found out would do everything they could to assist us in passing the test if we showed that we knew something about the subjects. This intimacy, of course, doesn't exist with the present system.

• • •

For many years United States Lines dry-docked its ships in shipyards throughout the United States. Many factors determined where, at what time of year, and for what reason. Often schedules would be the deciding reason, when cargo on a certain trade route was slack, for example, or if coast guard or American Bureau of Shipping surveys were due, an empty ship could be examined more quickly and thoroughly than one where the inspectors had to climb over and around cargo to examine interior plating and the internals of tanks. Weather also played an important part in determining the shipyard period. If known welding repairs had to be carried out, or if the hull had a big accumulation of grass and barnacles, cleaning and recoating were much more efficiently accomplished in warm weather than the dead of winter.

After many years of dry-docking in American ports, the company made the decision to dry-dock overseas where the costs were considerably less than the States, in spite of being required to pay a 50 percent customs duty. No duty was levied if the overseas dry-docking was for safety reasons or emergencies, however. The American shipyards usually had resident coast guard inspectors stationed in the yard or in the port so any required inspections could be scheduled by a simple phone call to the Marine Inspection Office.

Overseas dry dockings required the company to pay the expenses of sending two inspectors, a hull inspector and a machinery inspector, to the foreign port, as well as pay for their meals and hotel accommodations. Dry dockings in the Far East usually were handled by inspectors from the coast guard office in Hawaii, and European dockings were covered by inspectors from east coast cities.

I was sent to Korea on one occasion for a routine dry-docking of one of our freighters and requested that the coast guard dispatch two inspectors to the yard. Upon my arrival I met them. One was from Hawaii, but the other was from a coast guard office on the east coast. This surprised me because of the extra travel involved, but they informed me they were the only ones available at that time. The hull inspector was a man with whom I had worked before, and we got along very well, but the machinery inspector was new to me, as well as to the hull inspector, and was considerably younger than the hull inspector.

I met the inspectors that afternoon in the yard prior to the ship's arrival, at which time we reviewed our work procedures. I noticed the machinery inspector was wearing a new pair of safety shoes and remarked how well they were made. He told me he had just purchased them in the safety store in the Korean shipyard and he further informed me that this was his first inspection overseas and only his fourth vessel inspection since he had been in the coast guard. He had been schooled in vessel automation and that's why he was dispatched to this job. He added that he didn't own any safety shoes and that being a safety inspector it would only be proper that he purchase a pair to wear on the job. He seemed very pleased with his new shoes and pointed out their features to me as we talked. They had deep cleats on the soles, were especially made of a synthetic material to resist oils and greases and still maintain traction on a wet steel surface, came up over his ankles for additional support, and sported instep protectors and steel toe caps to prevent injury from anything that might fall on his feet. Finally, they had a built-in elastic section which would enable him to kick them off quickly should anything such as hot molten metal land on them! I got the impression he was attempting to show me how much better Korean safety shoes were than those made in the USA!

We boarded the ship after it docked that evening and introduced ourselves to the captain and chief engineer and told them of our schedule for inspections while in the yard. We ate supper on board and the two inspectors left for their hotel. I stayed aboard for another half hour to line up some paperwork and then left for my hotel.

I boarded the ship the next morning and the hull inspector boarded shortly after. He told me the machinery inspector was on the pier and asked me to go out on the pier to speak to him. I thought he had already discovered something on our hull to which he wanted to call my attention, so I hustled ashore accompanied by the hull inspector.

As I approached him I discovered he was leaning on a pair of crutches and his foot was bandaged!

"What happened to you?"

"When I was leaving this ship last night, I crossed over from the ship's gangway to the large steel accommodation platform furnished by the shipyard and the deep cleats of my safety shoes got hung up on the last tread of the steel ladder and I fell forward and sprained my ankle!"

As sympathetic as I felt, I had to work to stifle a laugh!

"I won't be able to do your inspection, but I'll tell the hull inspector what to do and we'll get through it okay. It won't be necessary to call for another inspector."

This being his first time overseas, he certainly didn't want to have to return to the States without having done some sightseeing and shopping, I gathered.

We proceeded with the inspections and everything went well for the next several days. I found that I was staying in the same hotel as they were, so we got along very well, with me filling him in on the day's activities each evening. On the third day, the young machinery inspector asked me if United States Lines had an office in the port and I told him we didn't, but any correspondence to me from the company would be mailed to the estimator in the yard to my attention and I would receive it at once.

I asked why he wanted to know and he told me he had been talking on the phone with his wife the night before and that she had baked some cookies for him and wanted to know the address to send them to him! Holding back a laugh, I told him to have her send them to the same address I used. The cookies arrived a few days later, but were just a box of crumbs!

The ship left the yard the same day he had the cast removed from his ankle, so he and his new safety shoes left for home the next day!

On another occasion I was putting a ship through a coast guard inspection in New York and attempting to soothe the machinery inspector after he found a few petty problems, such as an occasional drip from the packing gland of a fuel pump creating a small puddle of fuel in the containment tray beneath it. It would be routinely wiped up, but it gave him something with which to find fault. He also discovered a small cover plate missing from an electric switch, claiming a man could put his finger in the hole and get a shock. Of course, I wanted to tell him if a guy was stupid enough to do that, he deserved a shock, but I held my comment.

The chief engineer, Eric Seim, was accompanying us on the inspection and was getting just as peeved as I was at him, but I told Eric to cool it and we'd get through it okay.

The inspector then asked us to start up the idle generator in order to test the over speed trip of the turbine driving the generator.

Eric opened the saltwater valve to allow cooling water to the lube oil cooler prior to starting the unit, but a stream of saltwater squirted from between two flanges, so he secured the valve. He said he had instructed his new third assistant engineer to renew the gasket the day before, but it was obvious that the man had not tested it after the renewal.

The inspector remarked, "Boy, he must be some engineer!" This remark was all Eric needed at this point and he blurted out, "Well, you people licensed him; I didn't!"

This irritated the inspector and I thought we'd never get through with this. I told him we would correct the problem and the generator would be ready for a test when he returned in the morning. The next morning a different inspector appeared on the scene, a man with a better temperament, and we breezed through the remainder of the inspection.

Because inspections required so much time in port and would occasionally delay the sailing of a ship, particularly when longshoremen were ordered for an eight o'clock start in the next port, it was suggested that the company and coast guard experiment for one trip by having two inspectors ride a ship from the east coast of the United States to the west coast and perform the various tests underway.

The company would permit each inspector to bring his wife aboard; they would occupy the passenger quarters and eat in the officer's dining room. When this was proposed to the inspectors, we were told the commander in charge of assigning inspectors was overwhelmed by men volunteering for the job. They looked at it as two weeks away from the office, only one ship to inspect, a sightseeing trip through the Panama Canal, liberty in a Panamanian port for a few hours, and a free flight home from the west coast!

The company expected the ship to be fully inspected during this voyage and completely free of any requirements when it docked on the west coast, but such was not the case—by a long shot! The hull inspector was on the bridge constantly, looking over the shoulder of the captain and mate on watch, asking questions about their navigation and ship handling, and generally being a pain in the neck. Whenever the mate would have a lifeboat prepared for inspection the inspector would examine it, or test fire hoses or countless other safety equipment on deck, and at the end of the trip the mate ended up with an armful of deficiencies which had to be taken care of before the ship could sail from the West Coast to the Far East. Many of the requirements involved purchasing new gear on the West Coast when we had the same equipment in our storeroom in New York!

The machinery inspector caused a similar disturbance in the engine room while underway. He was constantly pointing out such minor problems as a small leak from a fuel pump or fire pump packing gland, peering over the shoulder of the second assistant engineer while he was testing boiler water, or checking on the purity of the water being produced by the ship's evaporators.

The reports from the ship at the end of the voyage were enough to convince the company that the experiment was a dismal failure. The captain and chief engineer pleaded with the company to never burden them again with such a foolish escapade, the two inspectors were always in the way on the bridge and in the engine room during maneuvers entering and leaving port, and particularly during the delicate passage through the Panama Canal!

During the canal transit, a minimum of people are allowed on the bridge because the captain, pilot, and mate are constantly running from port to starboard checking lock clearances and line handlers on the pier and lock. The inspectors and their wives were promptly told to leave the bridge at this time and their feathers got ruffled at this!

• • •

As I stated earlier, each United States Lines and Pacific Far East ship which left the States for Japan would fuel to capacity when possible, depending upon the amount of cargo carried. The determining factor would be the ship's Plimsoll marks, which would indicate the maximum draft at which the vessel could leave port legally. After loading its cargo, enough fuel would be loaded to bring the ship down to the marks for the waters in which it was to be navigated.

The SS *Pioneer Ming* was discharging its inbound cargo at a commercial pier in Honolulu one time and management had scheduled a fueling operation concurrently with the cargo operations. Calculating the draft at the completion of discharging and loading of cargo was an easy figure to reach and this draft would dictate the amount of fuel we could take to bring us down to our marks at sailing time from Hawaii.

The vessel also carried several tons of military cargo to be discharged at Pearl Harbor upon completion of the commercial cargo operations. The schedule called for the ship to be shifted from the commercial pier to Pearl Harbor, which would require the ship to leave the commercial harbor area and proceed outside into the Pacific Ocean for a distance of between one and two miles and then to reenter the military area of the harbor.

Because the vessel would be considered to be in the Pacific Ocean for a fleeting moment between harbors, the company requested a waiver from the United States Coast Guard captain of the port for permission to allow the ship to leave the commercial area below its marks during the two miles. This would enable the company to load nearly another thousand barrels of fuel at the commercial pier, and then, after the Pearl Harbor cargo was discharged, the ship would be even with the required marks for sailing to Japan.

The company explained to the coast guard about its fuel-holding tank in Japan as a money-saving effort benefiting two American shipping companies because of the high cost of fuel in Japan. The company also explained that fuel barges were not allowed at the loading pier in Pearl Harbor due to the fire hazard, therefore the fuel had to be taken aboard at the commercial pier during the earlier cargo operations. The coast guard was unsympathetic to the company's request and denied the waiver, thus costing the company several thousand dollars. The vessel might have slipped away from the commercial area unnoticed and back into Pearl Harbor without repercussions; however, it wanted to stay within the law. At sailing time from the commercial dock and also when leaving Pearl Harbor, a coast guard officer was seen on the pier reading our draft, probably because we called their attention to it!

• • •

Our container ship, the SS *American Lark*, was tied up to a pier in Antwerp, Belgium, discharging cargo on a sunny afternoon, when suddenly the skies blackened, a severe wind blew up, and a torrential rain came down in a matter of minutes. Everyone on the pier ran for cover in a nearby shed and the operator in the crane discharging our ship climbed from his gondola and started to descend the steel ladders in a hurry to seek cover.

Normally, idle cranes are anchored to their tracks when not in use, but the idle crane next to ours broke its anchor bolts when caught by the hurricane force winds and was driven down the track until it collided with our crane, whose boom was extended out over our forward hatches. The two cranes began their run along the tracks propelled by the wind until the wheels of our crane jumped the track and the crane collapsed on the *American Lark*.

The force of the crane resting on our ship pushed the forward end of our ship away from the pier, causing our bow lines to part and swing the ship into the river until it was nearly perpendicular to the pier. At that moment a small self-propelled river barge was passing and saw the *American Lark* swinging into its path, so it gradually eased itself against our ship and gently pushed it back to the pier and held it there until shore personnel and the ship's crew could put out more mooring lines. When the vessel was secure the captain of the barge waved good-bye and disappeared!

No one thought to get the name of the barge, and to this day no one knows who saved our ship and several other barges which were in the path of the swinging ship from untold damages! The *American Lark* suffered a great deal of damage from the crane collapsing on it, the port-side lifeboat was demolished, the radar mast was destroyed, the radio antennae were torn loose, and the handrails were destroyed on the flying bridge. I was sent over from New York to survey the damage with underwriters and put repairs in hand to make the vessel seaworthy to return to the States.

Because of the damage to our safety equipment, it was necessary to notify the United States Coast Guard as well as the American Bureau of Shipping of the casualty. Our company agency called the local ABS office and our New York office called the coast guard in New York. The coast guard told us they had a coast guard commander in the area at that time and we could have him appear to sight the damage. Our agency located him and informed him of our needs. He appeared the following morning and informed us he was there for an investigation of another matter, and also that he was not a marine inspector! I informed him that we couldn't wait for a marine inspector to be sent over before starting repairs and, with or without him, we were starting them. The American Bureau of Shipping surveyor, a Belgian, stepped into the discussion and came up with the solution.

He told us he had the power to act on behalf of the coast guard under certain conditions. The captain of the ship, the ABS surveyor, the coast guard commander, and I would be required to go to the office of the United States Embassy in Brussels and inform the consul of our plight and he would take it from there.

The consul was fully knowledgeable of the routine and he swore in the Belgian ABS surveyor to act in behalf of the United States Coast Guard in this situation, in the presence of a high-ranking United States Coast Guard officer! I shook my head in disbelief. How was this possible? Everyone laughed at my attitude, but I told them that all I was interested in was getting the ship repaired and on its way home, whatever it took.

A large life raft was purchased from a local ship chandler, radar repairs and antennae repairs were completed, railings were repaired, and the ship was on its way in a few days. The ABS surveyor issued a Seaworthy Certificate, signed the United States Coast Guard bridge card, made an entry in the official logbook on behalf of the coast guard, and everything was legal! At sailing time I thanked the ABS surveyor for his assistance and then thanked the coast guard commander, but I don't know why!

The crane operator who attempted to escape from the moving crane realized it was in a collision situation with the other crane and jumped from the second landing of the crane to the ground and suffered a broken leg.

There was a good possibility the owner of the river barge, which stopped the swinging of the *American Lark*, would have been in a position for compensation or even a minor salvage claim if he had identified himself, but a search for him by our agency proved futile.

• • •

When sewage disposal units became a requirement aboard American ships, our ships under construction were no problem because the machinery could be added in the engine room during their building. The company was then granted a grace period for the installation in the company's older vessels.

I boarded one of the older ships which was assigned to me just after it returned to New York from Philadelphia and docked in Staten Island. Its sewage disposal system had just been installed on the voyage before and tested and passed by the United States Coast Guard and American Bureau of Shipping surveyor at the time.

While I was in the engine room looking over the plant a man approached me and identified himself as a United States Coast Guard inspector and stated he was there to check on the operation of the sewage plant. I informed him that the unit had been installed a month before and had been fully tested and approved by the coast guard and, if he wished, I could show the approval document to him.

He replied, "I know it's new, but we are spot checking these new installations to be certain the crew is using them while the ship is in port. Now, can you have it demonstrated for me? I've never seen this type."

"Yeah, sure," I replied, "but it's a waste of our time just after our arrival in port when we are quite busy!"

I called the chief engineer and told him of the situation, and he agreed to explain its operation to the inspector. While explaining it, the inspector asked, "Is that pump over there part of the unit?"

"Yes, it is," the chief replied.

"Well, why isn't it running?"

"The unit isn't calling for it to operate at this point."

"Well, I want to see it run. How will I know if it does or not?"

"There isn't any reason to run it now, inspector."

"RUN IT!" he insisted.

The chief pressed the starting switch, the pump turned over for a moment, and then the chief stopped it.

"Oh, no, let it run for a while."

The chief again started it, watching a gauge carefully, and after a few minutes said, "I have to stop it now; it's losing suction," and he stopped it.

The inspector then asked, "What is the purpose of that pump:"

"I just pumped four days' worth of sewage overboard into the harbor from the holding tank, inspector!"

"You what?"

"Yeah, you told me to!"

The inspector looked at me and I shrugged my shoulders and said, "He's right, you told him to!"

I reported the incident to our office and the company waited for any repercussions, but nothing ever came of it, so apparently the inspector thought he had better leave well enough alone.

• • •

On another occasion, before sewage disposal units were required, I was standing on a pier with a coast guard inspector inspecting the exterior of one of our ships' hulls when a gush of water flowed out of an overboard discharge and into the bay. He remarked, "This ship is designed wrong; that toilet overboard discharge shouldn't be located there. It will run into the lifeboat if the boat is in the water." I told him the ship was twenty years old and I doubted that it was designed wrong. If it were, that fact would have been discovered before then.

I told him that particular overboard discharge was from a freeing port on the main deck, a type of drain to relieve excess water and prevent puddling.

"It sure looked like a toilet overboard to me," he replied. I told him to stand by on the pier and I would prove it was not a toilet overboard, and then boarded the ship. I went to the purser's office and borrowed a bottle of ink and then knocked on the door of a crew member whose room on the main deck was located above the questioned overboard discharge.

A lady whom I assumed was a waitress answered the knock and I told her I had to check her toilet. Seeing the United States Lines logo on my coveralls she admitted me and I entered her bathroom with her following me. I poured the bottle of ink into her toilet, rushed out of the bathroom, and shouted out her porthole to the inspector on the pier to watch the overboard discharge. She spoke little English and looked bewildered at this nut dashing around her room. I went to the main deck and asked the inspector if he had seen the ink. He replied that he had and he was satisfied that the discharge he had seen earlier was not from the toilet.

Later, I overheard the waitress talking to another crew member in Spanish and pointing toward me. I could imagine what she was saying; "That weirdo came to my room, poured some black stuff in my toilet, and ran out shouting to a guy on the pier!" Talk about extremes we had to go through to prove a point!

• • •

In 1961 Tom Wilhelmsen and I were working aboard one of our ships as port engineers finishing up a coast guard biennial inspection at our company piers in New York. It was Saturday night, about 5:00 P.M., and only one test remained—the setting and sealing of the port boiler safety valves.

Our coast guard inspector was one of the old-time inspectors left over from World War II, when civilian inspectors were put into the coast guard, and he was biding his time until retirement. Our plan was to have the crew light off the idle port boiler during the night and have steam up on it by Sunday morning, ready for the setting and sealing of the four safety valves. Upon successful completion of this the ship would leave New York on its European voyage.

I walked to the gangway with the inspector that evening, and on the way he hinted that a bottle of Scotch whiskey might ease us through the inspection on Sunday morning!

Setting and sealing safety valves can often be a cliff-hanger because one or more of the valves could behave erratically, fail to lift at the prescribed pressure, fail to blow down properly and cleanly, or fail to reseat itself, any one of which would be cause to delay the vessel's sailing for up to twenty-four hours while the boiler was cooled down, the faulty valve changed, and the entire drill repeated.

With this in mind, I agreed to the whiskey bribe—anything to get the ship out on schedule! When I arrived home that night the liquor stores were closed, so I put one of my personal bottles in my briefcase for the next morning.

The following morning, Tom and I were in the chief engineer's stateroom changing into our coveralls when Tom removed a bottle of Scotch from his bag and told me the inspector had told him the previous night that a bottle of Scotch would be greatly appreciated on Sunday morning, sort of a "thank you gesture for making the inspector work on a Sunday"! I opened my bag and showed Tom my bottle and we had a good laugh to think that we were both approached!

The inspector appeared and Tom and I gave the bottles to the inspector separately so he wouldn't suspect we had talked it over. We went through the safety valve drill while the inspector stayed in the chief's office and listened to the valves popping off in the engine room! We returned to the chief's office and the inspector remarked how clean they sounded. He gave the lead seals to Tom and me, we went below and sealed the valves and then returned his seal to him, and he thanked us and left the ship.

Tom and I were changing our clothes when the chief engineer asked, "How do I recover the cost of the two bottles of Scotch the inspector hit me up for last night while you were down below? After you left the ship, I had to run ashore and buy two bottles for him. I gave them to him while you were in the engine room this morning!"

When Tom and I left the ship that morning we decided we had better tell our boss of the liquor incident, so on Monday morning we told Bob Lurye. He told us he would discuss it with the higher-ups in the company and the following day he told us in the future to call him, at home if necessary, and he would handle it. The situation never occurred again as far as I know, but I often wondered just what the company would do if it had. After all, the company's unwritten rule was "Don't let anything delay the sailing of one of our ships!"

• • •

It wasn't long after this incident that I was going through another biennial inspection and the inspector had just finished sealing the safety valves when I invited him to eat dinner aboard the ship before leaving for home. The seal used by the inspectors is shaped like a pair of pliers, and when squeezed against a lead seal leaves an imprint with his coast guard number impressed in the lead. Two small copper wires are weaved through the lead and through the adjusting arrangement on the valve, thereby preventing any tampering with the adjustments. The inspector laid his seal down on the dining room table, ate dinner, said his good-byes, and left the ship. The ship sailed for Australia. The dining room waiter was cleaning up after dinner and found the seal and thought it was just an ordinary pair of pliers and put them in a drawer in the dining room with the silverware!

In the meantime, the inspector realized a few days later he was missing his seal when he was dispatched to another job and, retracing his steps, recalled he left it on board our ship. He made a frantic call to the company office and, quietly and in confidence, told our boss of the situation.

The boss contacted the ship's chief engineer at sea and a search of the dining room turned up no seal. No one thought to ask the waiter if he had seen it! A few weeks later, the waiter was cleaning the silverware drawer and noticed the "pliers" and told the chief engineer that someone had left them in the dining room while the ship was in New York a month earlier.

The chief sent a radio message that the seal had been found and now the company wanted to inform the inspector about locating it, but how to tell him without his principals finding out? I called the inspector on the phone and informed him of the discovery and he breathed a sigh of relief. He informed me that he had been borrowing the seals of other inspectors for the last month and was dreading that his superiors would find out! The chief airmailed it back to the office and I called the inspector to come over to our office and he was presented with his seal. I didn't dare volunteer to deliver it to him because my presence in the coast guard office would prompt questioning from someone there!

Any future inspections by the inspector on company ships were a piece of cake!

UNITED STATES CUSTOMS

The Name's the Same

In 1953 and 1954 the government built a group of new general cargo ships and made them available to private shipowners and operators in an effort to upgrade the American flag merchant fleet. The ships were known as the Mariner class. They were twenty-knot ships and were operated for the government during their guarantee period by many companies, and then offered for sale to the companies at the termination of the guarantee.

The companies that wanted to operate them realized these ships were ideal for upgrading their fleets; however, they felt the asking price for them was prohibitive, thus the new ships headed for the lay-up fleets around the country, after only six months in operation. As time wore on, the companies kept a close tab on their value as they were depreciating at periodic intervals. When their price reached what the companies thought was reasonable, many companies put in their bids for their purchase, including the United States Lines. The company wanted to purchase nine, but the government only allowed them eight, relinquishing the ninth one to the American Export Lines.

I was assigned to the SS *Gopher Mariner* as first assistant engineer, and left for Newport News Shipbuilding Corporation where the vessel would be towed from the James River lay-up fleet. The ship was well preserved while laid up and required a minimum of work to reactivate it. One of the work items issued to the shipyard was to change the name of the ship to SS *Pioneer Minx*.

The eight Mariner-class ships the company purchased were to be renamed using the name *Pioneer* as the first name and the second was to be a four letter word beginning with an M to distinguish these ships by class from others in our fleet. The American Pioneer Line was a shipping company absorbed by United States Lines many years prior to World War II, and its trade route was the Pacific Ocean, the same route the new Mariner-class ships would be traveling. These ships were to be named after some of those earlier Pioneer ships. At one time the letters AP were painted in the white bands of red, white, and blue company colors on the smokestacks, but was eventually discontinued when our Far East customers began to confuse our ships with those of American President Lines, a west coast shipping company which also had trade routes in the Pacific.

The name *Gopher Mariner* was located on the port and starboard sides of the bow and across the stern of the ship. Each letter making up the name was cut from steel plate, one-half inch thick, and was twelve inches high. These letters were welded in place and then painted white. Changing the name of a ship should be a routine formality which involves notifying the United States Customs, a few forms, and having a customs officer view the change.

United States Lines informed the customs office in Newport News of its intention to change the name, completed the required forms, paid the required fees, and then gave the shipyard a repair order to begin the change. This would entail a great deal of labor because a staging had to be built at each bow and over the stern to support the workmen and their gear used for burning the welding off the letters of the old name, grinding the residual weld clean from the hull, and cutting in the new name in block letters with a bead of weld forming each letter. By outlining each new letter with a weld, a permanent pattern would be in place for each time the hull would be painted in the future and relettering the name would be easy. The company elected to do this for economical reasons instead of remanufacturing new steel block letters as originals. Because we had sufficient time in the yard to accomplish this, the name changes in all three areas did not take place concurrently, but were done one at a time to utilize the same equipment and manpower. Upon completion, the new name was painted in using white paint and looked quite impressive against the black hull. This entire process took more than two weeks to accomplish.

On Monday morning we called the customs official for the port and informed him we had completed the burning and welding and we would like to have the name changed officially that date. When he arrived at the pier, he sighted the completed job and immediately took exception to it.

"Why wasn't I called at the time the name was changed instead of after the fact?" he growled, obviously upset.

We explained the elaborate program we have gone through to change the name, but he insisted he should have been called at periodic intervals to witness it.

We reached a compromise with him by agreeing to have the shipyard furnish a large piece of heavy-duty craft paper laid out in the paint shop of the yard; the yard would paint, in twelve-inch block letters, the name *Gopher Mariner* as it had appeared originally on the ship, and then tape the paper to the port and starboard bows and around the stern, covering the name *Pioneer Minx*!

This operation took a good deal of time, so the name change date was now wrong on all our forms and had to be modified to reflect the new date. Subsequently, he reported to the ship, and with a flourish the paper was torn from each bow and the stern area while he announced, "I hereby declare this vessel to be renamed *Pioneer Minx*!"

He signed the required documents, gave us copies, and left the ship. The captain said, "I was going to give him a bottle of company whiskey until he made us go through this useless charade." I remarked, "It's probably a good thing you didn't; he might have noticed it was bonded liquor and fined you for not having it locked up under seal!" Nick Bachko, the port engineer on the scene, declared, "Yeah, and he lost out on a lunch I was planning for him."

To a customs man, that would have been particularly painful, because they are known to appreciate a free meal, if not in a restaurant then at least aboard ship. When a ship is in port, try to find a spare seat in the officers' dining room at mealtime!

RECREATION

After World War II, while the company was establishing its trade routes to Europe, Australia, and the Far East, it became obvious that crew monotony was a factor to be dealt with on long trips at sea, particularly the twenty-three-day trip from Panama to Australia. Morale was something to be considered, lest boredom override the conscientious efforts of watch standers and day workers. To make these long voyages more enjoyable the new C-2-class ships were fitted with record players and radios in the crew and officers' dining rooms and, in later years, television sets and eventually VCRs on subsequent vessels.

The record players could only play 78 RPM records, which the crew and officers usually brought from home. The life of a 78 was quite brief, particularly if someone attempted to play it at sea and the ship took a slight roll! The record ended up with a few additional grooves and was no longer playable.

When televisions arrived on the scene, officers and crew would chip in to purchase them until the union contracts came up for renewal, at which time the unions asked the company to include them in the new contracts, which the company did. New black-and-white sets were installed in each mess room, but problems soon arose because every man who owned a TV at home became an expert at tuning them; thus when the vessel arrived in port a TV repairman was always called to realign the sets and restore them to normal performance.

A couple of years later, again when the union contracts were up for renewal, color TV was the rage, so the unions requested the company furnish color sets. An agreement was reached which stated "a color TV set will be exchanged for the black and white set, provided the black and white set is declared beyond economical repair." Not long after one of our ships arrived in New York from Europe and the officers' black and white TV was found to be beyond economical repair, so a color set was installed. The crew then requested their sets to be changed to color, but the company cited the union contract and told them their black and white set was still suitable, and the ship left on its European voyage.

On the return voyage home, a disgruntled crew member threw the black and white set overboard just before their arrival in New York in the belief that the company would be forced to install a color TV upon arrival. The company took a dim view of this attitude when informed of the circumstances and refused to install a color TV, citing the wording of the contract, "...that the black and white set shall be 'replaced' by a color set." Obviously they couldn't 'replace' a set that didn't exist! It was a bitter lesson in semantics which lasted for one voyage and then the company installed a new color set for them.

VCRs were the next luxury to be installed; however, they were not the conventional household type, but instead used a different size videotape than the household units. The reason for this was to keep the crew members from stealing the company-furnished tapes, but it also prevented the crew members from bringing their own tapes to be played on board, which upset the crew immensely. It wasn't long after that the manufacturer of these VCRs went out of business and company resorted to the conventional VCR and everyone was happy.

Another form of recreation encouraged by the company was baseball. On the ships running to Australia the company provided uniforms with the name of the ships embroidered on each one. Games were played ashore with teams in Australian cities and in some Japanese ports. Ships on the European runs did not have uniforms, but many ships still fielded teams and played in England and Belgium. Our teams usually lost because of the lack of practice facilities on board, since playing catch was the only practice to be had. Even this would usually use up several balls each trip, lost overboard when a man missed a catch. Often, the day after a game, the players on our team would be hobbling about with sore arms and charlie-horsed legs because of lack of exercise.

While playing a game in Antwerp against the marines from the United States Embassy in Brussels, our second assistant engineer suffered a broken arm while pitching, and on another occasion a crew member broke his ankle stepping into a recessed rail track on the pier while chasing a fly ball! Still, the company encouraged playing sports.

Captain Tony Gallo was one of our more enthusiastic captains and always encouraged the crew on his ship to get out on the pier and throw the ball around and was usually calling ahead to our agents and offices to ask them to line up a game for his ship's team.

While our ship was tied up in New York on one occasion, he was in uniform and he and I were having a cup of coffee in the officers' dining room when a new crew member reported aboard. He was a young man, about twenty-five years old, and asked for the chief engineer.

"I'm the chief engineer."

"I just came from the union hall. I'm the new oiler," he said.

"Okay, let me have your assignment letter."

He produced a letter, and while I was reading it, the captain asked, "You play ball, young man?"

He replied, "You play ball with me, captain, and I'll play ball with you!"

He left the dining room and we had a good laugh over his remark, but he turned out to be a "lover" while ashore rather than a ball player.

THIEVERY

Ships seem to have an affinity for thieves. For some strange reason many people have the idea that anything on board ship which is exposed is there for the taking. People who would never entertain any thought of stealing something ashore think nothing of helping themselves to materials on board a vessel.

When a ship ties up to a pier many people clamber aboard the moment the gangway is lowered. First aboard are usually customs officers and public health officials, followed by company representatives who may include a port captain, payroll department people, and a port engineer, plus longshoremen, vendors, repair contractors, and ship chandlers, and, most importantly, a company watchman who will be stationed at the gangway. Of course, not all or necessarily any of these people are there to steal, but with such a large boarding in such a short time, the temptations are there, and it is almost impossible for the watchman to check identifications or for the officers and crew to police the ship. The customs and immigration officials usually request a private boarding until their work is completed and once they "clear" the ship, the others swarm aboard.

The many public spaces on board offer untold opportunities for theft. Places such as the crew and officers' lounges and dining rooms which might contain VCRs, clocks, televisions sets, and radios, plus the engine room machine shop with its tools and the bridge with its clocks and binoculars are all easy pickings for thieves.

The crew and officers attempt to keep these spaces locked, but this security is short-lived because vendors, repair people, and others with legitimate business in these areas must have access to them and thus they are unlocked shortly after the vessel's arrival at the pier.

Usually the officers and crew will not steal because if caught it means immediate dismissal and the individual's name and identification are entered into the files of the Marine Index Bureau, a clearinghouse accessed by shipping companies to learn the backgrounds of prospective officers and crew members.

As an example, one time a crew member removed a ship's striking clock from a bulkhead in the crew lounge, packed it in his suitcase, and left the ship, his relief trip finished. As he passed through the company pier gate at noon, the clock struck eight bells, calling attention to himself. A search of his bag by the company watchman and a customs guard revealed the clock and the man was detained for further action and his name and seaman's identification number were recorded in the Bureau where his reputation would be forever on record.

Another area which is exposed is the galley. Though not exactly a public space, it is usually located in an area on the main deck while the ship's walk-in refrigerators are located one deck below. The galley is often left unattended while the cooks and utility men leave the area to pick up groceries from the storerooms and refrigerators. Upon their return they find their carving knives, cleavers, and sharpeners missing. This is especially painful to them because often the cooks will bring their own personal knives aboard, preferring them over those supplied by the company.

A classic case of theft occurred aboard a tanker which had just entered Newport News Shipyard for its annual repair period years ago. The ship's steering wheel in the bridge was a fine example of intricate woodworking with inlaid segments of colorful exotic wood. Obviously it was too nice, because after the second day in the yard, the captain reported it missing from its steering stand. The port engineer reported the theft to the shipyard security department and they took charge of the investigation to find the thief, alerting the guards at the gates to search all vehicles leaving the yard; cars, trucks, railroad cars, and small craft.

The following day the wheel was found hidden beneath an old tarpaulin which had been haphazardly thrown over it in an area reserved for junk and waste material. The port engineer was informed of the find and he requested the yard replace it at the binnacle as soon as possible and the wheelhouse would be kept locked thereafter.

The shipyard security force, however, had other ideas. They asked the port engineer to give them a few more hours to attempt to find the thief and then pointed to a man sweeping in the area of the tarpaulin.

"That sweeper over there is really one of our security men who is on surveillance duty and he's waiting for the thief to make his move and he'll arrest him," a security man told him.

The following day the wheel was still under the tarp and the port engineer pleaded with the yard to forget the detective work and just put the wheel back where it belonged, but the yard insisted on catching the thief and requested more time.

The next day the port engineer noticed a painter working nearby, later a maintenance man, and then an electrician, all whom he assumed were security people, so he felt somewhat relieved that they were keeping an eye on his wheel.

A few more days passed until the day before sailing, and still no culprit, so once again he asked them to put his wheel back in place. As the yard was preparing to abandon their watch on the wheel, a forklift operator carrying a huge piece of machinery, his visibility limited by the large load, drove over the tarpaulin and demolished the wheel!

The yard had to quickly fabricate a new temporary wheel and mount it in place for the ship to leave the yard on time. In the meantime, the shipyard ordered a new wheel from the original maker and installed it when the ship returned from its next voyage. The thief was never found!

On another occasion, on one of our older ships, the anchor chains on each side of the bow were condemned by regulatory surveyors and new chains were ordered for replacement the following trip upon the return of the ship from its next European trip. When the vessel returned to our company pier in Manhattan, the old chains were removed and lowered to the pier where they were to remain until a scrap salvage barge could pick them up.

The new chains came alongside on a lighter and were installed, the anchors were bent on, and testing was completed. The ship sailed on a Friday and the old anchor chains remained in two piles on the pier for a weekend. On Monday, the port engineer on the job, Charlie Higgins, went to the pier to direct the loading of the old chains onto the salvage lighter and discovered the chains were gone!

Each chain was nearly thirteen hundred feet in length, weighed several tons, and made two piles ten feet across and five feet high. The chain was on the apron of Pier 62, which also housed the operations department of the company, and was probably the best watched and guarded pier in the company.

Who stole the chain, with round-the-clock watchmen on duty only a few yards away but saw nothing? Probably an inside job, but no one was talking. As some officials said later, "What the heck; it was only scrap anyway!"

My ship, the SS *Pioneer Ming*, was tied up to the company pier in Manila, Philippines, one time, and we were discharging huge sections of steel pipe, four feet in diameter and twenty feet long, to be used for an aqueduct in the outlying districts of Manila. The pipe was carried as deck cargo due to its size and to expedite its discharge. Eleven sections had been discharged without incident, but the last one slipped from its slings and dropped into the water between the ship and the pier and sank to the bottom of the bay. The water was about forty feet deep there, so our office manager decided to continue working cargo to prevent any delay of the ship and send divers down after the vessel left port to put lashings on it to recover the huge pipe.

We later learned the divers went down and reportedly couldn't locate it, even though it had fallen directly beside the pier! The company collected insurance on the loss, but everyone was convinced the divers had received a better offer from others and it would eventually be recovered, maybe at night, or some weekend when there was no pier activity!

• • •

Ever since prohibition was repealed in the 1920's, United States Lines has been in the whiskey shipping business, answering the call of the liquor-starved populace of America. The company won contracts with some of the largest distillers in Scotland and held onto them up to World War II and continued thereafter.

The whiskey trade grew rapidly after the war and the company concentrated on having a sufficient number of ships to accommodate the busy trade at the expense of other trade routes. It was also a good run for crew members because it was a reasonably short trip compared to other routes, and there was plenty of time in good liberty ports of the United Kingdom. Whiskey is an extremely lucrative cargo, and each ship was charged with safeguarding it, not only during its carriage, but also during loading and discharging operations: Anyone caught pilfering it or attempting to smuggle it ashore was subject to immediate dismissal, whether a crew member or longshoreman.

The company provided additional watchmen in addition to the ship's officers to prevent pilferage during the loading and discharging; however, when you have sixteen to twenty cases loaded on a pallet, suspended from a cargo hook, and it comes aboard in swinging fashion, it could "accidentally" land heavily against the vessel's structure and there are bound to be a few broken bottles!

In the days following World War II, a longshoreman would hold the job of providing drinking water to the men working cargo. He would lower a bucket and ladle into the cargo hold and the men would help themselves to the water. Of course, it was painful for these workers to see the whiskey leaking out of the broken bottles and into the ships bilges, so they would use the ladle to catch it, but before all the stevedores in the hatch had time to enjoy a swig from the ladle, the flow from the broken bottle(s) had stopped. There had to be a better way!

Citing the unsanitary method of obtaining drinking water from a common ladle, they requested the company purchase a new type of water carrier with a tight lid to keep out dirt, and a small spigot instead of a ladle and, most importantly, a tubular paper cup holder attached to the cooler's side. This provided each worker with his own cup for the prevention of spreading germs. Of course, it also provided him with his own container in the event of any spillage!

I was aboard one of our ships in Glasgow when a longshoreman managed to conceal an entire case under a winch and get it off the ship after dark during the supper hour. He had learned that the ship's engineers had to send a pump ashore for repairs, so he conspired with a crew member to conceal the case in the box containing the pump. The whole operation was well planned and went off without a hitch. When the van carrying the box reached the machine shop in the city, the case was transferred to a car and the mission completed. At least they thought it was, but the longshoreman hadn't done his homework.

For every batch of whiskey cases loaded aboard, one extra case containing labels only is loaded. Where that case of whiskey had broken earlier, some of the labels on unbroken bottles might be washed off by the leakers, thus the consignee of the whiskey would have spare labels to replace them. The case stolen by the longshoreman was the case of labels for that batch of whiskey, and he became the laughingstock of his stevedore gang for his stupidity!

• • •

On one occasion while I was on a whiskey ship as third assistant engineer, the chief mate found a few unopened bottles of Scotch concealed beneath a winch on deck after sailing for New York, so he passed them out to various officers, rather than making out a claim and report. He gave a bottle to me, advising me to transfer it to another container if I still had it upon arrival in New York. I accepted it and thought I would give it to one of the port engineers who handled the ship when we arrived in New York, but customs inspectors boarded the vessel on arrival at the pier so I had to get rid of it quickly. I had an empty, brown, quart bottle which had previously held a medication called Brown's Compound. The purser had given it to me earlier when I had asked him for one to hold photographic chemicals.

I quickly poured the Scotch from its bottle to the brown bottle and threw the Scotch bottle overboard. A few minutes later, a customs searcher knocked on my door for a routine search of my quarters. As he gave the room a quick look, he saw the bottle in my bathroom on a shelf. He picked it up, read the label, and said, "Oh, Brown's Compound, I know what that is. That's okay!" I breathed a sigh of relief, because if he had studied the label a little more thoroughly he would have seen, "Contents 1,000 tablets" on the label!

It was a stupid gesture on my part because I didn't drink and I ended up pouring it down my toilet. When I had time to give it a serious thought, I wondered how I could have offered a drink of expensive Scotch to anyone from a brown bottle.

Many of the whiskey ships were fitted with huge cargo oil tanks built into the structure of the hull as a section of the cargo hold. If the company received a booking for a bulk cargo oil such as tallow, lubricating oil, tung oil, latex, or any others they often carried, the shipper could be accommodated. Rarely did the company find it necessary to turn away cargo. Their unwritten rule was, "If we book it, we'll carry it!" Of course, our eager salespeople made all sorts of promises to shippers, often without consulting the marine department to determine if we had the facilities to carry their goods!

These cargo tanks were designed to carry dry cargo as well as bulk liquid and were fitted with large covers which could be unbolted and hinged to enable whiskey in cases to be loaded into them. When the compartment was full, the covers were lowered down into position and bolted and the whiskey was thus safe from any pilferage, especially since more cases were loaded on top of the covers.

At least it was thought to be safe! The inboard sides of the tanks formed a common bulkhead with the shaft alley adjacent to the engine room. Fitted into these bulkheads were bolted manhole covers, accessible from the shaft alley. These were used for entry to the tanks for installing temporary cleaning gear and chemicals to clean the tanks once their liquid cargo was discharged. On one of the early voyages carrying whiskey after the war, some engine department personnel were believed to have opened one of the cases, because when the longshoremen discharging the ship got to that level in the tank, that broached case was discovered. Of course, no one knew how it had happened, but from that point on a welded bar was fitted across the covers and a seal applied to the manhole cover.

• • •

Many of the waterfront bars in European and Far East ports sport a nautical décor, probably to attract the seamen from the ships of the many companies and nations who call at the ports. One decoration which seems to be very common to every bar is a life preserver from each ship which calls at that port. It is not unusual for the bar owner to offer a free round of drinks to a group from a ship calling at his bar for the first time, in exchange for a promise of a life ring the next time they are ashore. These preservers are valued publicity for the bar owner because they are stenciled with the vessel's name and hailing port.

Of course, the spare life rings, as they are also called, are locked up in a deck locker, so the crew member who has made the promise merely lifts one out of the life ring rack mounted on deck near the gangway and walks off with it! This is another situation where everything on deck which isn't locked up seems to be there for the taking. Even the American flag flying on the ship's stern in port is fair game and has been reported stolen in a few cases!

LOVERS

The SS *Pioneer Ming* was a turbine-driven ship powered by two high-pressure steam boilers. These boilers were fired with liquid fuel pumped from tanks through heaters and strainers and then through a tubular burner which had a sprayer plate in its end to atomize the fuel for combustion. The sprayer plate is a nickel-sized flat disc with a precise orifice drilled through its center, and its size determines how much fuel is sprayed into the furnace.

While a ship is tied up in port, small sprayer plates are used, because without the main turbines in operation, the load is reduced. Larger size plates are installed in spare burners by the fireman to prepare for a heavier load on the boilers when the ship leaves port and heads to sea.

On one occasion, about an hour before leaving Japan for the States, the fireman on watch informed his watch engineer that the rack which held the larger size plates was empty. A search of the fireroom was made and the sprayer plates were indeed missing. I was in my office finishing last-minute reports when I received a phone call from the engineer telling me about the missing plates.

Fortunately, I had a spare set in my office. I rushed them to the engine room, the fireman installed them and the vessel left port on schedule. Without them, the vessel would more than likely have arrived on the west coast behind schedule due to its reduced speed.

At some time during the next twelve hours, the missing sprayer plates turned up in their rack and were put into service, but no one seemed to know where they had come from or at what time they were returned! Of course, someone knew and we later found out through the grapevine that one of our three firemen had fallen in love with a

143

young lady he had met in a bar a few days before the ship was due to leave and this was an act of desperation to force the ship to remain in port another night!

We had no way of proving this, but the suspect left the ship when it arrived in New York. He had been a relief man and the man he relieved returned from vacation and the problem never arose again!

• • •

When a ship leaves the States on an extended voyage to the Far East the crew settles down at sea to a routine, standing watches or performing normal duties on day work, and then, off watch or after five o'clock many enjoy hobbies, watch movies on a VCR in the crew or officers' lounge, reading, or just having a gab session in someone's room. Homesickness sets in occasionally, but most men are acclimated to the lonely life of a sailor, knowing they will be home with their loved ones eventually.

Some, however, cannot seem to wait to get home to their loved ones, preferring to enjoy the favors of a loved one in each port! Such was the case one time in Honolulu when my ship, the SS *Pioneer Ming*, had docked on a Sunday afternoon and one of the engine department crew went ashore to seek a companion. He was due to report to work on Monday morning at 0800 but failed to do so. The first assistant engineer reported his absence to me as I was leaving the ship to go ashore to do some shopping. I arrived at the pier gate just as a taxi pulled up, and as I stepped toward the cab its door opened and my man started to get out, drunk. He saw me and apologized for not being at work, and I told him to report to the first assistant and then go to bed and sleep it off, but not to go to the engine room.

The cab driver told him he owed him $7.50 for the ride. The crew member, in his drunken state, told the cabbie he had gotten sick in his cab, but didn't want to throw up on his upholstery, so he held open the top pocket of the Hawaiian shirt he was wearing and threw up into it. The cabbie appreciated this but then the drunk said, "But that's where I keep my money!" Then he reached into his pocket and drew out several single dollar bills dripping with vomit!

"I don't want that," the cabbie said disgustedly.

"I don't want you to take it either," I said. "I'll pay for his ride, here's $10.00; keep the change," and I told my man he owed me ten bucks and he'd better remember it when I returned to the ship later that day.

The following day I brought him before the captain who "logged" him a day's pay for failing to report for duty. Logging is the usual penalty for such an infraction because the company must pay another crew member to perform the missing man's work. The captain enters the man's name in the official logbook, a coast guard document in which the crew members' name, ratings, dates of employment, infractions, pay amounts, and other pertinent data are entered, and then turned over to the coast guard at the end of the voyage.

Another logbook on board is found in the engine department and is a large, bound, hardcover book about fourteen inches square. When opened out, it becomes a large spreadsheet, nearly newspaper sized, which contains several columns with headings in which are entered the temperatures and pressures of all machinery in use in the engine room.

Because of the numerous entries to be made each hour, the pages are quite full, leaving only a small box at the bottom of each page of any remarks to be entered for such tasks performed on each watch such as pumping bilges, starting the fire pump to put wash down water on deck or washing mud from the anchors and chain when heaving in the anchor, testing the watertight door, or unusual sounds from the high-pressure or low-pressure turbines. Because of the limited space for these remarks, I required the engineers to abbreviate where practicable, such as W. T. Door, for watertight door; W. O. Deck, for water on deck; H. P. Turbine, for high-pressure turbine; L. P. Turbine, for low-pressure turbine, and F. B. Drill for fire and boat drill.

One evening one of my engineers went ashore from the *Pioneer Ming* in Yokohama to have a few beers in a bar. While there he met a young "bar girl" and she suggested they go to a "love hotel" nearby. She informed the engineer he would have to pay the *mamasan* so many yen to release her for the evening because she would no longer be able to solicit drinks. He agreed and the two left in a taxi.

When they arrived at the hotel, the Japanese desk clerk required payment in advance and insisted they fill in the room register. Not wishing to give his correct name, the engineer thought quickly and wrote in Mr. and Mrs. H. P. Turbine, telling his girl the H stood for Harry! He left the room a few hours later to return to the ship to stand his watch.

The following morning, while the ship was still in port, the shore side telephone at the ship's gangway sounded and was answered by the Japanese watchman. It was the young lady calling from the hotel and asked to speak with Mr. H. P. Turbine, probably to be sure he had made it aboard okay the previous night. The watchman, who spoke very limited English, asked her what department Mr. Turbine worked in and she replied, "Engine Department," so he came to my office to inform me of the call.

"Mr. Chief Engineer, telephone call at gangway for Mr. H. P. Turbine," he said.

Trying to stifle a laugh and keep a straight face, I replied, "Mr. Turbine went ashore a few minutes ago to do some last-minute shopping."

"Okay, Mister Chief Engineer, I tell her!"

I never did find out which engineer was Mr. Turbine. Later at a department safety meeting I asked who Mr. H. P. Turbine was and no one volunteered, but one man did say, "I've never heard of H. P. Turbine, but I know a few W. T. Doors, F. B. Drills, and W. O. Decks!"

• • •

In another love hotel incident one of our crew members met a young lady in a bar and, as in the previous incident, paid the *Mamasan* to take the girl from the bar to a hotel. He wore very thick eyeglasses and after registering at the desk he and the girl retired to a room which was located in the middle of a long corridor with ten to twelve rooms on each side.

The room numbers on the doors were very small for some reason, but wearing his glasses he had no difficulty locating their assigned room. Each room had a sink, but no bath, and a toilet was located at the end of the long hall on each floor. Also standard equipment in each room was a kimono for each occupant.

Early the next morning he awakened, slipped on a kimono, and left the room to go to the bathroom and left his door slightly ajar. As he opened the bathroom door he heard a door slam closed behind him, probably caused by a gust of wind from an open window in the bathroom. After using the toilet he returned to the hallway and soon realized the door slamming closed was to his room. Without his glasses, he now had to grope his way along the hall, peering closely at each door in an attempt to read the small numbers which were just a blur to him!

He thought how stupid it was to leave without his glasses, but then who needs glasses to go to the toilet! He tried to recall just how far he walked to the toilet and finally decided which room it had to be. He was quite sure he had selected the right one when he quietly opened the door and saw a young lady sleeping alone in bed. Not wishing to wake her he slipped off his kimono and crept into bed with her.

Suddenly, awakening, she let out a scream! He tried to calm her, but, without his glasses, now wasn't sure he was in the right room! She leapt from the bed in her kimono and ran out into the hallway, still screaming. He threw his own kimono back on and followed her into the hallway.

With this uproar, girls and guys began rushing from the other rooms, and the desk clerk, who had been dozing at the front desk, came rushing into the fray attempting to straighten things out. Our guy was suddenly grabbed from behind by his girl and she told him not to say anything.

"Do not speak; I know all these girls. I explain!" she said.

A lot of Japanese words were thrown around while our guy stood dumbfounded! As it turned out, he had missed his room by one door, but the young lady he disturbed was found to be a girlfriend of his girl and she did not have a date that night and was just spending the night alone in the hotel. When it was straightened out, everyone had a good laugh over it except a couple of people who complained about being awakened so early!

To smooth things out, the hotel management gave everyone a free bottle of Saki, and then charged our guy for it!

• • •

During World War II our armed forces conducted many types of training courses to educate the young men who were to go forth in different theaters of war. Among these were training films used to show the potential dangers of venereal diseases. My brother-in-law, Fred Collagan, starred in one of them while he was in the air force. After a brief interview and audition, he was selected from eight others in his unit to be a doctor in one film, mainly because he was able to pronounce the big medical terms more readily than the others. They became the "patients" and had horrible-looking scabs, ulcers, and open wounds painted on their bodies to illustrate the ravages of the diseases.

Also, the military set up prophylactic stations in many cities in the vicinity of known houses of ill repute. One such "prostation" was set up in Antwerp, Belgium. Soon after the allied forces liberated the city, United States Army medics moved into the city and selected a small building in the city's red-light district to be its medical headquarters for venereal disease prevention.

After a GI was to leave any house of ill repute, the only route available to him to return to the street was through an aid station where he was handed a prophylactic kit to be used in the privacy of one of its rooms. The kit contained two tubes of salve, plus a small cotton bag to be tied over his private parts and held in place with a small drawstring. The purpose of the cloth bag was to prevent staining his trousers from the salve. GIs call the bag a Bull Durham bag because it resembled a small bag once used by a tobacco company as a container for its pipe and cigarette tobacco. After using the pro kit he was ushered to an exit in the street.

One afternoon two men and I went ashore in Antwerp from my ship and were walking along the sidewalk next to the outlet door of the treatment building and noticed two GIs leaving. One of them began walking slightly behind his buddy, pointing downward to the shoes of his friend and calling everyone's attention to his buddy's feet.

The cloth bag used by his friend had apparently slipped loose and fallen down his pants leg and was hung up on his shoelace, and his friend was having a good laugh over it at his buddy's expense as he dragged it with him. We followed them for about a block watching others on the sidewalk break out laughing when they noticed it.

While the two continued walking, an army captain approached them coming from the opposite direction. The GI dragging the bag saluted him, but his buddy was preoccupied with calling people's attention to his friend and did not see the captain. When he failed to salute, the captain stopped and admonished him for failing to salute an officer, but then he spotted the bag and broke out in laughter. Any efforts on his part to maintain his composure after that fell apart. So much for military decorum!

• • •

On one of our trips to the Far East the SS *Pioneer Ming* arrived in Yokohama from Hong Kong on a Friday afternoon. Cargo discharging operations began upon arrival and could take about two days, after which we were to leave for three other Japanese ports for discharging and reloading before heading back to Yokohama to top off our cargo and then head homeward.

At our first call at Yokohama one of our engineers met a young lady in a bar and they fell in "love." He told her of the ship's schedule and that he would be returning to Yokohama in about ten days so they made plans to go on a picnic in the mountains at that time. The schedule was such that the ship would return on a Friday and remain in port for two days.

There was only one snag to his plans—he had a watch to stand in port plus some boiler maintenance to do at that time. He asked me (make that pleaded) if he could have the two days off if he worked extra hours during the ten days and had the boiler maintenance completed by our arrival back in Yokohama.

I agreed to this, provided he could get another engineer to stand his port watch at that time. He was an excellent engineer and a pleasure to work with, so I had no problem giving him the time off and I knew he would have no problem finding another engineer to take his watches. At sailing time his girlfriend was on the pier waving goodbye to him and he told her at that time to make the plans for the picnic.

The ship left port, made its call in the three ports, and returned to Yokohama on schedule, and he took off with his girl who was waiting for him in a taxi on the pier. When he returned two days later just prior to sailing for the States, he came to my office to report he was aboard and to thank me for the time off. He then handed a gift-wrapped package to me, saying it was a present from his girlfriend.

I opened it and was surprised to see a beautiful kimono with my initials embroidered on it.

"She was so grateful, chief, that you gave me the time off that she wanted to show her gratitude. She made it during the ten days we were gone between ports. She made one for me, too!"

I stood there looking at it while my mind jumped ahead a month when I would be showing it to my wife and trying to keep a straight face as I explained the circumstances surrounding it! When I did get home, I showed it to her, and after examining it closely she said, "This is homemade!" It was at this time I told her the story behind it.

She remarked, "I believe you; no one could make up a story as good as that, but..." I guess that was her way of saying, "I believe you!"

A few years later, I was sent to Taiwan to handle the dry-docking of one of our ships. The officers and crew members remained aboard the ship during the six days in the yard while I had a room in the Kingdom Hotel, one of the nicer hotels in Kaoshiung. Once again, one of the engineers fell for one of the local beauties from a bar, and stayed at her place during the vessel's stay in port.

At the completion of repairs the vessel left for Japan and I remained in the city for a few more days waiting for the shipyard to gather its timesheets and material lists to prepare an invoice for me to use in negotiating the costs of the work. Most shipyards all over the world work in this manner; they bid on the work to be done from specifications submitted to them, and then rely on the extras for making additional money, using the excuse of necessary overtime to complete the work—the machinery was worn worse than it was made out to be in the specs, the underwater areas of the hull had a lot more rust and scale than we anticipated, etc. What it comes down to is the fact that we would hand our ship over to them for repairs and maintenance for six days, they would repair it, and, on completion, the ship would leave their facility. We would then argue about the cost of doing the work. No auto repair garage or home builder would ever do business in this manner!

I was two days in the hotel awaiting the call to start negotiations when the hotel desk called me to meet someone in the lobby. *At least,* I thought, *now we can get on with it and I can head for home.* Instead, when I entered the lobby I saw the girlfriend of the engineer sitting in an easy chair. I looked around for my negotiator, ignoring the girl when she called to me, "Mr. Port Engineer!"

I walked over to her, sensing all eyes from the hotel employees were on me, because most of the "business" girls are known by hotel employees.

"Mr. Port Engineer, I made this for my boyfriend from your ship. Can you take it to America for me and send it to him?"

She opened her bag and took out a pretty pillow about fourteen inches square and four inches thick. It was truly beautiful, and I told her so, but at the same time I didn't have the heart to say no, so I accepted it and assured her I would send it to him, even then knowing it would not fit in my suitcase. Its bulk was not what really worried me, however. As she left the lobby, I made it a point to say goodbye in a formal manner, in a feeble effort to impress the hotel help that I was merely acting as a courier, and not a paramour!

I returned to my room admiring the pillow when I discovered she had installed a zipper on one side, so I removed the thick piece of sponge, threw it in the waste-basket, and folded the cover to fit neatly into my bag. I wasn't about to send it to the engineer when I returned home because I didn't want to play the role of house wrecker!

When I returned home, I emptied my suitcase on my front porch, a habit most of us learned early in our careers; you never know just what strange insect life from the Far East may have decided to take up residence in your clothing! My wife was sitting on the front porch watching me unpack when she spotted the pillow cover. She picked it up, remarking how pretty it was, and then said, "It looks homemade!"

Immediately, my mind went into reverse a couple of years to the kimono, as I told her the story behind the pillow.

"Uh huh? Just like the kimono from two years ago, huh?"

I thought she must have read my mind!

"I can't send it to the guy's house; he could be married," I blurted out.

She replied, "You better not; this is beautiful; I'm keeping it. I'll go to the store tomorrow and buy a piece of sponge for it. It'll look good on our living room couch!"

And there it sits today.

• • •

All the lovers were not seagoing types, however. One of our ships was laid up, out of service, in a shipyard in Baltimore, while we awaited word from the government that it would be accepted for the lay-up fleet in the James River in Virginia. The shipyard had tied up the vessel at its most remote pier at the far end of the yard. The ship was completely shut down, with only a single power line from the pier to the shore power outlet on deck to power a few lights on board.

The only person permitted aboard was a watchman who was an employee of a shore watchman service with whom we had contracted, and he was stationed at the gangway to prevent anyone from boarding in an effort to prevent theft. A shipyard engineer made a daily round on board to assure the vessel was secure and not developing any leaks, etc.

One Saturday evening at about ten o'clock the engineer heard loud music emanating from the direction of the ship, so he walked aboard and discovered a rollicking party going on! The ship's watchman had brought a record player aboard, found the keys to the passenger lounge and passenger rooms which were adjacent to the lounge, and was allowing his "guests" to use them. The yard engineer counted more than fifteen people on board having a wild time. Extension cords were in use everywhere, all receiving their power from that single power line from the pier. They were cooking hot dogs and hamburgers on a charcoal grill they had found on deck and beer bottles and cans were strewn everywhere!

He kicked everyone off and called the local office of United States Lines in Baltimore. We changed watchman services after that!

• • •

After World War II many seaports in Europe and the Far East faced a massive rebuilding effort in order to restore the pier areas where the cargo could be loaded and discharged after having been hammered by enemy planes and ships. While the city fathers planned the rebuilding to restore the cities' economic being, entrepreneurs were contemplating the possibilities of prosperity along the waterfront.

Knowing that soon peacetime cargo shipping would begin and the import/export trade would be booming, these people bought up run-down stores, cafes, storerooms, and warehouses along the street adjoining the pier area and built new restaurants and bars in their places. Also, aware that most of the first ships to dock there with peacetime cargo would be Americans, the new owners chose names familiar to their crews. Names such as Texas Bar, Boston Bar, Time Square, California, and New Jersey were a few of them. Some even offered a free beer if you could prove you were from the place for which the bar was named.

A few bars left over from the war were rebuilt and retained their original names, such as Claire de Lune, Zanzibar, and Robot Bar, all to be found in Antwerp. In English cities, the British retained the original names of their pubs, and although many had been destroyed by Axis bombs, the dogged Brits were not ones to let a minor thing such as a war dampen their drinking spirits.

One popular name used there was the Red Lion, a café which seemed to be found in nearly every major British city. I have even seen a Red Lion in Hong Kong when it was under British rule. As a matter of fact, I dropped in there one afternoon to have a cold beer while shopping and was approached by a Chinese "lady of the evening." She could obviously tell I was an American from the American ship anchored in the harbor. She asked, "You in the NMU?" (NMU stands for the National Maritime Union and represents the crews on the United States Lines ships.)

"Why?" I asked.

She then slid the side of her split Chinese skirt aside and revealed the initials NMU tattooed on her thigh!

I laughed and said, "No, I'm in the MEBA." (Marine Engineers' Beneficial Association)

She slid the other side of her skirt aside and there it was MEBA!

I laughed at this and asked, "What if I told you I was in the MMP?" (Maters, Mates and Pilots)

Then she laughed and said, "I have that tattoo also, but you have to buy me a drink if you want to see that one!"

Needless to say, I didn't buy the drink, but she did give me her business card which read Hot Pants Molly Malone and it included her telephone number in Hong Kong. The other side of the card had Chinese writing on it and I never had it translated.

When I returned home, my boss in United State Lines confiscated it when I showed it to him. I know he got a lot of laughs with it!

• • •

When I first walked ashore in a British City, I was confused by some of the signs in the store windows: Casket Opening, Monday; Casket Closing, Thursday; and Players Please and soon found out the lottery in Britain and Australia is called "the Casket," and the days mentioned were the first and last days for play. Players Please was not the gambling café I suspected, but the name of a popular brand of English cigarettes.

Later, while in a British elevator (or rather a lift), I wanted to get off at the second floor and pushed 2 on the floor selector and a lady behind me told me that was the banquet floor and it was closed at that time.

"Where do you want to get off?" she asked.

I told her my room was on the second floor, and she repeated the banquet story again.

"My room is one flight up from the lobby," I said.

"Then you are on the first floor!"

"No, I'm not; I know what floor I'm on. My room's on the second floor!"

By now, she was becoming somewhat trying when she asked, "What are you, a Yank?"

"Yes, I am!"

"Well, no wonder; you're going to have to learn proper English if you want to get along in our country; the correct name for the floor just above the bottom floor is properly called the first floor, regardless of what you Yanks choose to call it!"

I said, "Madam, if you ever get to America and stay in an American hotel, you're going to find yourself not only on the wrong floor every night, but maybe in the wrong room, and on second thought maybe that's what you need!"

We both got off the elevator and later, while standing at the bar, I saw her leave the hotel on her husband's arm. I hope she told him of our conversation; I think he would have enjoyed being there because it didn't appear to me that she was too much fun to be with!

HAMMERS

Although there are few nails aboard ship, a hammer is still a valuable tool on board. Of course, the carpenter still has his claw hammer; whether he may need it or not, it's still a necessary tool for him to bring aboard, if only to collect his "tool money"! Other hammers on board which seem to be in constant use are chipping hammers—those horrendous, noisy, nerve-racking demons which keep everyone awake from dawn to dusk with their staccato clack-clack of steel against steel! In recent years some ships have replaced them with rotary chippers, which are air operated and do a faster job of cleaning rust, but are no less noisy.

During World War II, my ship, the SS *Clara Barton*, had four chipping hammers in constant use by the deck department. To add to this noise some crew members would make rings out of two-shilling pieces by holding the coin on edge between the forefinger and thumb and pounding it on its rim with a hammer while held against the steel deck and rotating the coin. As its rim mushroomed from the beating, its diameter reduced, and when the width of the rim was from an eighth to a quarter of an inch, the center was drilled out, after a small amount of buffing with emery cloth, the ring was completed.

The combined noise of a dozen ring makers and the chipping hammers was sometimes unbearable. Strangely, the chipping hammers began to disappear over a period of time (certainly not thrown overboard by disgruntled crew members!) until only one remained and the chief mate kept that one in his room when not in use and only released it to whomever he felt was responsible enough not to lose it!

While the ship was tied up to a coal-loading pier in Cardiff, Wales, awaiting shifting to a loading berth, one of the deck department men was chipping the area of the hull in the way of the anchor while suspended from a boatswain's chair when he lost his balance and fell from the chair into the water below.

A crane operator who was unloading coal from an adjacent ship witnessed the fall and immediately shifted his coal bucket to the area where the man landed and lowered the bucket into the water and the man crawled out of the water into the bucket. The crane operator lifted him from the water and deposited him on the foredeck of our ship where the man clambered out and thanked the crane operator. Though soaking wet, he still held onto that last chipping hammer, shouting to the chief mate, "Look, Mr. Johnson, I didn't lose the hammer!"

Many of the crew refused to talk to this guy after that episode, citing the one legitimate opportunity to lose the last chipping hammer on board!

Other hammers used in the marine industry are test hammers, carried by coast guard inspectors, American Bureau of Shipping surveyors, port engineers, and some marine surveyors. A test hammer is a lightweight hammer, the head of which has a pointed end and a blunt end. It is used to bang on steel to test welds, determine steel thickness, chip off rust to view a section of steel, plus many other functions, some of which are sometimes unnecessary and cause only grief to the ship owner.

An example of this is when a coast guard inspector once put the pointed end through the aluminum hull of one of our lifeboats directly under the engine of the boat. He had been told by his superiors that this area of a lifeboat is a place for standing water from rain showers and cannot be drained, thus there's a good chance the area could be wasted. Instead of observing the area from the interior of the boat, he elected to bang on the area from the outside, thinking the boat was made of sheet steel, and, after enough pounding, was able to penetrate the aluminum.

The port engineer called the company office and the office called the coast guard office and had the inspector removed from the ship. Renewing the aluminum plate cost a considerable amount because it required removing the engine from the boat and reinstalling it upon completion of the plate renewal. Of all the aluminum plates on the hull, the inspector had holed the most expensive one for renewal!

Still on another occasion, I know of a port engineer who was aware of the poor quality of the plates in a lifeboat and informed the inspector of them and had already put the work in progress for renewal. But as a joke he had borrowed a toy plastic hammer from his son's junior tool kit and handed it to the inspector and asked him to use this one on our boat!

I also know of a port engineer who asked the coast guard if he could examine the hammer he was using. When it was handed to him, he threw it overboard! The inspector smiled and produced another from his bag! Test hammers were an expendable product in the industry and were always given out by the shipyard and repair companies, as were coveralls, as a courtesy to the inspectors and port engineers. As a matter of fact, if a port engineer were to attend to a ship which was dry-docked in a shipyard and the yard said they did not have any coveralls for him, he would usually appear the next day wearing the coveralls of a rival shipyard whose logo and name were usually embroidered on the back. Upon seeing this a set of coveralls would quickly be located for him which bore the name of the yard in which his ship was docked.

I ran into a comedy of errors one time over a test hammer. While in our office at One Broadway, we received a phone call that one of our ships, the SS *American Legion*, had landed heavily against the pier while docking in Norfolk, Virginia, and probably sustained underwater damage. I left the office for LaGuardia Airport to catch a flight to Norfolk, taking my briefcase which contained a few papers pertaining to the ship and a test hammer. Upon arrival at LaGuardia Airport in New York, I was directed to a gate for my flight and told to hurry because the flight was about to leave.

The gate attendant looked at my ticket briefly and hustled me aboard. The flight left and upon arrival at the first stop, Roanoke, I was told the next stop was to be an airport in Tennessee. I quickly left the plane and was then informed that the airline had put me on the wrong flight in New York. My flight was the next flight to leave the gate from which I had departed earlier! I quickly went into the terminal at Roanoke and informed the airline of their mistake and that it was urgent that I get to Norfolk as soon as possible. I then told them I would rent a car and drive, but they told me another flight would be leaving in an hour for Norfolk and it would be much quicker than driving. While sitting in the terminal, I observed the security system in place. The airport had just installed metal detectors and it was obvious they were still a novelty to the airport personnel because a large uniformed officer with a gun would pass through it at intervals causing it to alarm.

"It's working good, Sally," he would announce each time to the security lady who was searching bags before passengers would be allowed to board.

In about an hour, my flight was announced and I approached the security counter with my briefcase. I opened it for her and she picked up the hammer and in a loud voice announced, "You can't board the aircraft with this; it could be a weapon!"

The security guard came rushing over, hand on his gun, "Did I hear weapon? Where is it?"

She showed the hammer to him, and he agreed I could not board with it. I said angrily, "Lady, I'm boarding this flight, with or without the hammer. As a matter of fact, you can keep the hammer!"

"What will I do with it?"

"Lady, you shouldn't have asked me that; I'm too much of a gentleman to tell you!"

"Watch your language, mister," I got from the guard.

The woman asked for my business card and said she would send it to my office.

I made the flight and, upon arrival in Norfolk, rented a car, drove to the pier, and then hired a diver who informed me the lower section of the ship's bow was badly damaged, so I arranged to dry-dock the ship at Newport News Shipyard. I followed the ship to the yard and arranged for a shipyard pass for my car. When I informed the yard of the problem with the test hammer, they drew one from their tool room, Department X-19, and gave it to me, at which time I threw it in the car trunk.

After a busy day in the yard, I left to go to a motel, and as I passed through the gate, the security guard asked me to look in the car's trunk. I opened it for him and he picked up the hammer, and seeing X-19 stamped on it, accused me of attempting to steal shipyard equipment.

I couldn't believe it. How could so much happen to a guy over a simple hammer? When I told the yard officials about it they asked for the hammer back and returned it to me two days later chrome plated! When I eventually returned to my office in New York my original hammer was laying on my desk with a red ribbon tied around it! I still have both hammers.

THE WAR YEARS

After the Second World War I was assigned to the Far East run, from New York to Hong Kong, Taiwan, Korea, and Japan, places I had read about in *National Geographic* years earlier as a little boy, but never imagined I would someday be visiting. Having spent the earlier part of my career on the European run during and after the war, and having been accustomed to dealing with post-war Germany, I would now be confronted with the Japanese for a change. How much, I wondered, would it affect me?

After docking in Yokohama that first trip, I took a leisurely walk uptown to see the sights. As I walked along a wide avenue, I came upon an elderly shoe shine man sitting beside the sidewalk.

"Shine, meester?"

I stopped. "Yeah, see what you can do with these old shoes."

I placed my foot upon his box and he removed the polish, brushes, and rags and set up for what appeared would be a big production. While brushing off the dirt, he asked, "American shoes?"

"Yeah, can you tell?"

"Oh, yes, I spend time in the States. Where did you buy?"

"Boston, a city in Massachusetts."

"Yes, I know. You know where Boston Navy Yard is?"

"Sure."

"I work in a restaurant across street from main gate; you know where Newport News Shipbuilding Yard is in Virginia? I work there in restaurant, too, and in restaurant in Camden, New Jersey next to the New York Shipbuilding Company! I work in many cities in States," he continued.

"When did you return to Japan?" I asked.

"Early 1941," he replied.

Just enough time to feed the Japanese war machine with all the information he had gleaned from his shipyard contacts, I thought. *But then, look at him now; all that time devoted to his country, and now he is relegated to shining the shoes of the enemy.* Poetic justice? Who is to say?

"A"MERGENCY LIGHTING

The lighting inside the passageway and living areas of today's ships are usually fluorescent types, but on earlier vessels, particularly those operated with direct current in their electrical plants, the fixtures were incandescent and used a standard light bulb housed inside a glass globe protected by a wire guard.

Some of these fixtures were on a separate circuit from others, even though they would sometimes appear to be from the same wiring source; however, these received their power from an emergency lighting circuit while the others were from the vessel's regular lighting wiring. The purpose of this was to ensure lighting in the passageway should the main power fail from the engine room.

On today's ships these emergency lights are labeled with a small nameplate marked with an E to distinguish them from the regular lighting; however, originally they were not labeled, so the United States Coast Guard issued a ruling which stated, "All emergency lights must be labeled or stenciled with the initials for 'Emergency' to distinguish them from the other lights."

When United States Lines received the notice, the company issued a circular letter to each ship to carry out this requirement. I showed the letter to the first assistant engineer and told him to paint a small one-inch square with white paint in the vicinity of each emergency light, and after it dried, to stencil the letter for emergency in the white square, using red paint, to make a neat-looking job.

Later that day, he informed me he had finished and asked if I would like to check the job. I laughed and told him such a minor job shouldn't require an inspection, but later when I left my office for a glass of water at the water cooler nearby, I walked by one of the lights and noticed an A stenciled in red on white! I then checked others and found all of them with an A.

I called him to my office and asked him how he spelled emergency and he replied, "A M E R G E N C Y!"

I just shook my head, but before we could paint out all the A's and replace them with an E, the captain saw the A's and asked me what they stood for. He had been giving some of the engineers a hard time about wearing uniforms in the dining room and I just didn't want to give him something else to find fault with, thus rather than tell him my first assistant engineer didn't know how to spell emergency, I told him the letters indicated those particular lamps which used alternating current, and that we were following a letter we received from the office.

Strangely, he just nodded and went on his way! I couldn't believe he bought that story, but when he left the ship a few days later, we changed the letters to E!

FOODSTUFFS

Food delivered aboard American flagships for consumption by the crew and passengers must be inspected by the United States Department of Agriculture under the same rules as the food sold in stores in the States. The reason I mention for consumption by the crew and passengers is because on one voyage aboard my ship, the SS *Pioneer Ming*, we carried boxes in our refrigerated cargo spaces which were labeled in bold letters, CHICKEN PARTS, UNFIT FOR HUMAN CONSUMPTION, U.S. DEPT. OF AGRICULTURE.

This cargo, several tons of it, was bound for Hong Kong, so we quickly spread the word on board to be wary if one were to eat a meal in a Hong Kong restaurant and to stick to seafood!

One rule which the Department of Agriculture enforces states that when food which has been loaded on board in the ship's domestic refrigerators, and the vessel leaves the United States, enters a foreign port, and then returns to an American port, that food must remain on board until the ship leaves port again. It cannot be removed from the ship after re-entering the States. This often presented difficulties to the company because if a ship were to be laid up after a foreign trip because of lack of cargo, its remaining food could not be removed and reloaded aboard another company ship. I should add the word "legally" after that last sentence, because it was often done without the authorities knowing it!

The proper procedure is to inform the Department of Agriculture at the port where the vessel is to be laid up. Remaining food is to be then discharged into the Department of Agriculture garbage truck which is equipped with a fitting for attaching a steam hose and the food then steamed until it is destroyed.

When the company expects the ship to be laid up they will inform the captain to have all the food thrown overboard at sea prior to arrival, leaving just enough to feed the crew until the ship is shut down. I was sent to San Francisco on one occasion to supervise the laying up of one of our chartered ships and the usual message had been sent to jettison the food.

When the ship arrived in port, the captain informed me he hadn't obeyed the company orders in throwing the food overboard because he couldn't see all that good food going to waste with so many people in need of it!

Fortunately, I hadn't yet informed the Department of Agriculture of the ship's arrival or the company's plans for lay up; also, I had the same feelings as the captain about wasting the food, so I was somewhat happy about the situation. We quietly asked the people in our local office to find some needy people, and by the next day we were discharging hundreds of pounds of beef, pork, liver, chicken, and frozen food into unmarked trucks which sped off to places unknown to us!

The following day, with only a token amount of food remaining, I called the Department of Agriculture and told them we had a few pieces of remaining food on board, the company having told us to throw the bulk of it overboard prior to arrival in port. They showed up, towing a small steam jenny behind the truck, the food was loaded into the truck, the steam boiler fired up, and we watched the steaming process carried out under the watchful eye of a supervisor in white coveralls. It was pretty tough to maintain our composure and keep a straight face during the steaming process.

Food for the crew and passengers was purchased from food purveyors and chandlers from reputable sources in the States, the company having a contract with several vendors in many different ports. After a long time at sea, some of the fresh fruits and vegetables would be rather soggy in spite of their having been under refrigeration, so when a ship arrived in port the chief steward would purchase fresh produce from these contract vendors.

On one occasion while my ship was in Australia, fresh fruits and vegetables were delivered and they were less than fresh, some actually rotten, yet the company was paying top dollar for it! Pleading with the captain to complain to the vendor, he said, "There is nothing I can do about it; this vendor is approved by our office in New York." He was correct, of course; our agent would not dare use any other vendor lest they lose their agency contract if they crossed the office! Our chief mate, Pete Strachota, was very verbal to the agent and captain, but to no avail. We did find out at the end of the trip that the vendors in Australia has been set up by a man who worked in the company office at One Broadway and who had been in the army stationed in Australia during World War II, at which time he set up this arrangement!

With this knowledge, Pete was promoted to captain, and when the vessel arrived in Australia, Pete went shopping and bought the freshest produce he could find and presented the bill to the agent. The agent shuddered when he thought what repercussions would be forthcoming from New York, but Pete stood his ground, the agent paid the bill, and the company was grateful to learn of the setup which had been going on for years!

Refrigerated cargos were always a headache for the engine department, because we were responsible for keeping thousands of dollars worth of exotic foods in good condition.

Australian lobster tails were one example, several tons of them to be maintained at 0° F. for over thirty days! Of course, one of the advantages of this cargo was the shipper would board the ship at the time of loading to meet the people who would be responsible for caring for his cargo and would usually give us a few cases of lobster tails for our own consumption! Whether this was to keep us from pilfering his cargo, or just a goodwill gesture of thanks for protecting it, we were never sure, but we never turned down the lobsters!

One of our new container ships arrived in New York carrying a forty-foot container loaded with five-gallon cans of pizza sauce from Europe. It was during the early months of our learning period for carrying various cargoes, a period when we weren't sure how much a forty-foot container could carry, weight wise or cubic wise. Because of its heavy weight the container holding the pizza sauce was loaded in the bottom of one of the holds, but in this instance this amount of pizza sauce proved to be too heavy for the aluminum container and the bottom of the container broke loose just as the container was lifted to the height of the main deck.

Hundreds of the five-gallon containers spilled to the lower hold, a distance of over thirty feet, and each burst open upon landing on the steel deck!

The lower hold was immersed in a red fluid about five feet deep. The broken container was removed and cleanup began. It was decided the obvious way to clean it was to use the ship's bilge pump to pump it overboard; after all, it was biodegradable! At the same time, the area would be hosed down and the cleanup completed.

Just as the pumps were started, a United States Coast Guard helicopter, on a routine patrol over the harbor, spotted the brilliant, crimson slick on the water adjacent to the ship and all hell broke loose. Police were notified, customs converged on the ship, and by now the word was a slaughter must have occurred judging by all of the "blood" in the water!

One of the inspections a ship must go through periodically is conducted by a United States Public Health Service surveyor. He routinely examines galley equipment for dirt, vermin, dishwasher water, and rinse water temperatures, storerooms and refrigerators for cleanliness, etc. I got to know the inspector who examined our ships in New York and would kid him once in a while about how clean we kept our ships, and he would always tell me he would find something wrong, and he always did! They tallied up their check-off sheets and a perfect score was one hundred. Our ship usually ended up with ninety to ninety-five, with minor infractions found, which were cleared up at once.

On one occasion I had just ridden a new ship from the builder's yard in Pennsylvania to our New York piers when he boarded. When I saw him I kiddingly challenged him to find something wrong on this ship because our building contract called for the ship to be clear of all regulatory requirements, including public health, and that one of his colleagues had just given us a clean bill of health the night before!

He laughed at this remark and said, "Just give me five minutes!"

He returned a half hour later with his report, at which time he said, "I gave you a score of ninety-nine."

I quickly scanned it and there it was—ninety-nine.

When the ship left the shipyard, new cutlery was put aboard in the officers' and crews' dining rooms and the chief steward, fearing it might be stolen while in port in New York, locked it up and left only a single spoon available for stirring coffee. He assumed the officers and crew would use the spoon and return it to a glass which contained water for use by the next person.

The report stated the coffee-time spoon water was cloudy and not being changed frequently enough! I told him I thought this was unreasonable and explained the reason for it, but he said, "How do I know someone isn't going to lick the spoon after using it?"

I asked, "Do you do that at home?"

"Sure I do, all the time!" and left the ship, grinning, while I was left holding his report in my hand.

• • •

When the United States Lines gave up its break bulk operations in favor of containerization in 1968, it also gave up its operations office and pier space at Piers 59, 60, 61, 62, and 76 on the west side, in the Chelsea district of Manhattan. Although it had a ninety-nine-year lease with the city of New York with several years left on it when they made the change, they made a deal with the city to take over the operation of Howland Hook in Staten Island, a new container terminal recently expanded by the city and looking for a tenant. Many city officials wanted to hold the company's feet to the fire to hold them responsible for the remainder of their lease; however, more level-headed city officials prevailed and the company pulled up stakes in Manhattan and a new lease was drawn up for Staten Island.

For several months prior to the changeover, the company had already entered the container business in a sense, carrying some containers on the decks of its general cargo ships. The Chelsea piers were ill suited to container-ship operation because of the lack of rail facilities and highways with easy access to the piers for the trailers. As a matter of fact, due to the lack of storage space at the pier, the company began storing its forty and twenty-foot containers along the center median on Twelfth Avenue beneath the West Side Highway.

This set up a ticket frenzy for the New York City Police, who hung multiple parking tickets on each container! Normally, after an automobile is ticketed in the city and is not moved from its parking spot within a few days, the city would tow it to a pound. They could not tow the containers away, however, because they were sitting on the street two and three high, and not on trailers! If the police had a ticket quota to meet, and I'm not suggesting they did, it was an ideal place to make their commitment.

When the company signed the contract to move its operations to Staten Island, amnesty was granted to the company for the tickets.

With the shift of cargo operations to Staten Island came a relocation for many office workers who formerly worked on the piers handling the paperwork, and the women who were transferred soon got labeled "Howland Hookers!" Today this moniker would not be tolerated, due to sexual harassment laws, but as I said earlier, it was a lot of fun while it lasted.

As a side note, when the company gave up the Chelsea piers, The United States Postal Department took over Pier 76 to house their mail trucks. At that time I was a committeeman for a Sea Scout group in New Jersey and I asked the company if they would contribute the remaining diesel fuel in our ground tanks at Piers 76 and 62 for use in our diesel-propelled Sea Scout boat. The tanks held several hundred gallons and were for use in the forklifts on the piers.

The company was very willing to donate it to us, because emptying them was one of the conditions of surrendering the lease. We drove in to the pier on a Sunday afternoon in a pickup truck carrying several fifty-five gallon drums. After emptying the tanks at Pier 62, and carrying it to New Jersey, we returned the following Sunday to collect the balance at Pier 76.

While pumping the fuel from the tanks there, we discovered an elaborate siphon assembly hidden beneath a tarpaulin not far from the mail trucks which were parked there because it was a Sunday, and next to the siphon was a large "Jerry can." It didn't take us long to connect the two—truck drivers would return their trucks to the pier area at the end of their shift, siphon some fuel from the truck to the Jerry can, and then pour it into their own cars. The arrangement was quite convenient because the drivers were allowed to park their cars in the spaces left when the truck was in use.

Needless to say, we "confiscated" the siphons and Jerry can and thus saved our government a lot of money and put a stop to the racket.

After our shift of operations to Staten Island, and the growing pains slowly ironed out, things began to run smoothly. New rules had to be observed, such as no pedestrians allowed on the roadways within the compound, passes or badges to be shown at the gate area to the guard while entering or leaving the compound, all packages searched entering and leaving, no private cars permitted on piers, etc.

In order to transport anyone, including longshoremen, to the ships at the pier, a quarter mile away, the company purchased an old school bus which would make scheduled runs between the gate area and the pier. The bus seemed to have a new driver each time I arrived at the pier and did not seem to be on any sort of schedule as far as I could determine.

I boarded one morning at the pier and sat down with several other passengers to wait for the driver. After about five minutes, I asked one of the others if he knew what time the bus was due to leave and he laughed, "They tell me the driver didn't show up this morning!"

"Well, who's supposed to drive us?"

"Anyone who knows how to drive a stick shift!"

"Hell, I know how."

"Then go ahead, mister; drive us."

At this point I thought I heard some groans from among those seated, perhaps because I was about to take them to work while they were already on the clock sitting on the bus! I climbed into the driver's seat and started the bus engine, and then shifted gears, but the diagram of the shift pattern, which is normally outlined on the shift knob, was worn smooth, so I had no idea where second and third gear were located, thus I drove the bus a quarter mile in first gear, about five miles an hour! I dropped off some of the passengers at the first ship and then moved the bus to the other ship, which was my destination.

I put it in neutral and climbed out after the last passenger left. A man climbed aboard after I left and asked, "What time are you going back to the gate, mister?"

"I'm not the driver; I'm going aboard this ship."

"Where is the driver, then?"

"Can you drive a stick shift?"

"Yeah."

"Then you're the driver, fellow; leave it at the gate," and off he went!

On another occasion a public health inspector drove onto the pier with a government car and parked it directly in the traffic pattern of the longshoremen who were driving tractor trailers to the loading areas beneath the loading cranes. The longshoremen told him he couldn't park there, but he became defiant and said that he was driving a government car and he could go anywhere he wished with it. Then he told them he would be about a half an hour on the ship and then he'd be leaving. The longshoremen called two tractor trailer operators to come forward and had them park their rigs directly behind and adjacent to his car to box it in, and the drivers then left to get more rigs.

He returned in a half hour and was livid when he found his vehicle hemmed in with no way of getting around the trailers. When he asked the longshoremen to move them, they told him they didn't know who had the keys and he would just have to wait it out! They "released" him four hours later!

The piers were quite efficient if everyone obeyed the rules, but often some people thought they deserved a little special treatment, such as the time one United States Lines employee thought it would be okay if he parked his brand new Buick close to the operations trailer, instead of the parking lot outside the gate area. He examined the cargo manifest in the trailer and then decided an area near where forty-foot containers were stacked four high would be free of any cargo activity for the day, and his car would be parked in the shade!

About noon, a tractor trailer broke down on one of the main arteries of the pier area, so all activities had to be rerouted on the pier. The containers were moved about the compound by a vehicle known as a straddle carrier, a piece of equipment which has huge wheels about five feet high and is capable of straddling a container and lifting it by its corner castings and carrying it to any location for pickup by the container crane. The operator of the carrier is in a capsule high up on one corner of the carrier and his visibility is extremely limited while driving this cumbersome rig.

Thus it was inevitable that, due to the detour on the compound, a straddle carrier carrying a forty-foot container began maneuvering in the same area where the Buick was parked. At one point the operator felt a slight resistance to his forward motion, and suspecting a pothole, reared the vehicle backwards a few feet and then gave it the gas!

One wheel of the straddle carrier rode up on the rear end of the Buick, flattening the rear tires, smashing in the trunk, blowing out the rear window, and wrecking the drive assembly to the rear wheels. Needless to say, the owner of the Buick was livid, but had no recourse to the company and had to rely on his insurance company to compensate him.

• • •

Vendors had permission to enter the cargo working areas at Howland Hook with their vehicles on weekends if the ship at the pier was not working cargo. This was often the case if a ship arrived on a Sunday afternoon. Vendors with repairs to be made on board could drive up to the ship's side and leave their vehicles there, since cargo operations were not scheduled to begin until 6:00A.M. the following morning. They usually made it a point to get their trucks or cars out of the area well before the 6:00A.M. start, however, or suffer the consequences!

On one occasion, a vendor had parked his car near the container crane, away from the side of the ship, and didn't move it for the Monday start, thinking it was in a safe area. The crane operator, not knowing there was a vehicle there, removed a massive hatch cover from the ship and transported it several feet to land it on the pier where it was normally stowed for the start of cargo operations.

The cover was gently lowered onto the vehicle and witnesses could see the car gradually being crushed to the pavement until it was like a pancake. By the time onlookers got to the alarm switch at the base of the crane, the damage was done. The crane operator had no visibility directly beneath when handling such a massive piece and had to assume no one would park a car there!

Vendors also had to be careful to park their cars only in designated areas, even though an area nearby may have had several cars already parked there. One vendor came to his car after completing repairs aboard one of our ships and found his car wouldn't start. He checked under the hood and found his battery missing and assumed someone had stolen it until a watchman told him all those cars which were parked there were being drained of fuel, batteries removed, and readied for shipment overseas in containers!

Two hours later, all the cars in the area were aboard ship!

THE IMPOSTER

In 1947 I was assigned to a vessel named the SS *American Jurist*, one of eight ships on the Antwerp-Rotterdam-Amsterdam run. I had been assigned as a temporary first assistant engineer for one trip while waiting for a new class of ship to be delivered within a month, at which time I would be assigned to one of them. At the end of that trip the new ships were not yet ready for delivery and I was asked to stay for another voyage. In the meantime, the chief engineer had accepted a shore position as port engineer in Baltimore and I was promoted to chief engineer.

While in New York the usual crew and officer replacements came aboard; men left for vacations, some men quit, some didn't care for the trade route, and others wanted a longer trip than the twenty-eight day turnaround of our ship. Among the new officers was a second mate named Harry Klitch, a man about forty-five years old. After reporting to the captain, he came to my office and introduced himself.

The relationship between the chief engineer and second mate on board ship is a unique one because they exchange information daily and each enters the other's noon report into their respective logbook. At noon, when the engine department logbook is delivered to the chief engineer's office by the third assistant engineer coming off watch, the chief does his daily accounting for fuel consumed, fresh water made by the evaporators, water consumed, and mileage made by the engines. This information is then placed on a company form and turned over to the second mate. The second mate records the day's run in observed miles (true) as well as the weather conditions for the past twenty-four hours, and furnishes the information to the chief for entry into the engineering log. The chief will also do some minor arithmetic using the observed miles and the miles made by the engines to calculate the slip of the propeller, and that information is then logged in each logbook.

Thus each day when Harry delivered the noon report to me he usually stayed around for a short time while we chatted. We became good friends and now that I had been assigned as chief engineer, I didn't want to leave for one of the newer ships where I would probably have to take a lesser job, the chief engineers' positions going to those with more seniority than I had. Harry had been assigned as permanent second mate and seemed happy in that position, even though he held a master's license and had previously sailed as captain.

We enjoyed going ashore together in foreign ports, eating meals and having a beer in unique foreign restaurants, and hanging out together on the ship. After having served aboard for about a year, and during our homeward-bound trip from Holland, he informed me that he realized there was no chance for promotion aboard the ship because the chief mate, Bill Hurley, and the captain, Jim Knowlton, were not about to get off. Even if Knowlton were to be transferred, Hurley would be in line for his job and Klitch would only become the mate, when he aspired to a master's position.

I had to agree with him. Just from our conversations and his obvious intelligence, it was easy to believe that he had more than likely held a master's job prior to his employment in United States Lines, although he didn't dwell on it, but I could understand his frustration. Thus he informed the captain that he would be leaving on the vessel's arrival in New York. He came to my office after payoff to say goodbye: I hated to see him leave, but was happy he was going back to the union hall to take his chances on getting a chief mate's job which might lead to a master's position.

In 1961 I was appointed as a port engineer in the company and was assigned a group of ships to supervise repairs and other duties to expedite the vessels' turnaround in port and prepare them for their next voyage. One of these ships arrived at our pier in New York a year or so later and I boarded it as soon as it was secured to the pier to begin my work and was walking up the foredeck when I saw Harry, dressed in dungarees and wearing a white sailor hat. He looked out of place, dressed as he was, since I had always seen him in a khaki uniform on board the *American Jurist*, but I approached him with my outstretched hand to say hello after many years of separation.

He saw me coming and, looking directly at me, shook his head with a "Don't acknowledge me" look on his face as I neared him! Bewildered, I merely walked by him and continued on my way to the chief mate's office. I discussed some of the deck department repair items with the chief mate and then asked to see a copy of the vessel's crew list.

Scanning it, I couldn't find the name Harry Klitch, so I stepped over to the porthole in the mate's office and saw Klitch standing on the main deck. I called the mate to the porthole, pointed out Klitch to him, and asked the man's name.

"Oh, that's Bob Bowker, one of my ABs. Came aboard last trip. The best sailor I have on deck. I'd like to make him the boatswain if the opening becomes available." I said nothing more, respecting Harry's silent request for privacy a few moments earlier. I saw him several times during the two days the vessel was in port, but neither of us acknowledged the other.

"Harry" remained on board as an AB for one year and since I was assigned to his ship, it was inevitable that I would see him every trip on its call in New York, which was nearly every five weeks, but each time our paths crossed, the standoff continued! And then one trip, I didn't see him and asked the chief mate about him.

"Oh, Bob got off last trip after payoff. His year was up and he was due for a vacation, but he told me he wasn't coming back. Something about seeking a better job, but he didn't go into detail."

Another year passed and I had not heard any more about Harry (or Bob) and then one day I boarded one of our new container ships, the SS *American Liberty*, and as I reached the top of the gangway, there stood Harry, in a khaki uniform and wearing two stripes, indicating he was serving as second mate. He had been securing the gangway just after the ship had tied up, and as I neared the top of the gangway he saw me, but once again gave me that shake of his head that had become so familiar to me a year earlier.

I simply walked by him and proceeded up an outside ladder to the chief engineer's office. The mystery was getting deeper and I was thoroughly puzzled at this point. During the vessel's stay in New York I ran into him a few times, but neither of us spoke. At sailing time I stood on the pier as the ship left and watched him standing on the stern supervising the stowing of the mooring lines. He looked down on the pier and saw me and he appeared to have a rather plaintive look when he saw me, but didn't wave or acknowledge my presence, and the ship left on its long voyage to the Far East.

The ship returned in three months and once again I waited in the dock office as the *American Liberty* was nudged to the pier by tugboats. Watching from a window in the office I saw Harry standing at the stern supervising the crew in putting out the mooring lines. After the vessel was cleared by officials and ready for cargo operations, I was first to board and, as I neared the top of the gangway, there stood Harry.

Once again, as so many times previously, I walked by him without any acknowledgement and started up the outside ladder heading for the chief engineer's office. I became aware of someone behind me using the ladder and then heard a voice, "George Murphy, my old friend, I owe you a long overdue apology!"

Stopping in the middle of the ladder, I turned and said, "Okay Harry, whenever you're ready."

We met at the top of the ladder and stood at the rail on the boat deck and gave each other a firm handshake and then a hug. He appeared to be somewhat drawn and tired looking, not the younger, spry man whom I had known so well years earlier. "To begin with, George, I'm not Harry. My name is Robert Bowker. Let me explain." And then the mystery began to unfold.

"When I was about nineteen years old I met a young man named Harry Klitch who possessed ordinary seaman's papers issued to him by the United States Coast Guard. He had made one trip to sea as an ordinary seaman and came to the conclusion that a life at sea was not for him. Having always had a yearning to go to sea, I took his papers and assumed his identity and registered in the crew union hall."

At this point I wanted to interrupt him and ask him some pointed question, such as,"Did Harry know you took his papers?" and "Did you ask for them or steal them," but I didn't want to cause him to lose his train of thought, and also he seemed to be in a hurry so I let him continue.

"After shipping out as an ordinary, I got my ABs papers and eventually became boatswain on a ship: The mates on there were very helpful and I began studying for my third mate's license, which I eventually received. I left the crew union and joined the Masters, Mates, and Pilots Union and registered for a job."

Again, I had more questions which I couldn't ask, such as, "How old were you at this time?" "What port did you ship from?" and "Did anyone know your true identity?"

He continued, "After a year of sailing as third mate, I had enough time for my second mate's license, which I obtained, and was fortunate enough to get a job out of the union hall and this continued until I finally passed my test for master. I sailed as master for a long time, but got married and left the sea for a while and then returned after a few years."

Now more questions were going through my mind, such as "Did you get married as Mr. and Mrs. Harry Klitch?" "If not, did you tell her of your identity?" "What about children?" but I let him carry on. He kept looking at his watch as he was talking and I told him I had all the time in the world to listen to his fascinating tale, but he said he was rushed, that his relief trip was over, and he had to get moving.

He continued. "Now we are at the time when I joined the *American Jurist*. Soon after I said good-bye to you I picked up a job through the hall as chief mate aboard a tanker and was subsequently promoted to captain. The tanker was on a scheduled run between Caribbean oil ports and Philadelphia, a rather short run but one which I enjoyed for several months because I could get home frequently."

After all these years, however, his charade was to come to an end one day when he was in the United States Customs House in Philadelphia to enter his ship, a routine procedure required of each ship entering an American port from a foreign port, when the customs clerk with whom he had been dealing with for many trips informed him of an "imposter" using Harry's name and identification number.

"Yeah, captain, he's an ordinary seamen aboard a ship which has been calling at this port for the last few months, and we noticed the similarity of names and ID numbers, so we plan to nab him when his ship returns on its next trip!"

Harry continued. "So I had no choice. I told the customs clerk that he was not the imposter; I was! The guy whose papers I was using suddenly decided to go back to sea and reactivated his documents. Somehow the similarity in names and ID numbers slipped through the cracks and he was granted the same papers he had held originally!

"The coast guard was called in and I surrendered my license and identification papers to them and awaited their action. They wanted to take my master's license away from me, saying I was using it under an assumed name, but my lawyer and I convinced them that I was the individual who passed the test for the license, regardless of who I was, and the most I had assumed earlier was the identity of an ordinary seaman.

"They took this into consideration and, as a penalty, broke me down to ordinary seaman and, as such, I would have to go to sea for one year and then would be permitted to sit for my master's license again!

"I had no choice, so I registered with the National Maritime Union, the same union I had belonged to when I started out, and got a job aboard a United States Lines ship, and that is where I was when you saw me on deck and I shook my head as a signal to ignore me. I just didn't want to get into a discussion at that time. Also, no one aboard knew me and I didn't want my background exposed.

"During my year as ordinary, I quietly studied for the master's license on my off hours and, when the year was up, I wasn't quite sure if I could still pass the test. My lovely wife encouraged me and gave me her undivided attention as she quizzed me on test questions and I reeled off the answers to her. When she was convinced I was prepared, she said, 'Go for it, honey!'

If it weren't for her support I would have given up. I took the test, passed it, and was awarded the license."

Now I had more questions which must remain unanswered, such as, "Did the coast guard continue your issue numbers on your new license or did they start them over from number one?" "Were you fined?" and "Were all the other certificates reissued without testing, such as radar endorsement and lifeboat certificate?"

"Anyway, George, here I am, and I'm glad to get this off my chest to you. You can't imagine the anguish I went through seeing you so frequently and not being able to say hello. I hope you understand."

"Harry, or Bob, let's get together sometime and continue this conversation; this is fascinating. I have a seabag full of questions!"

"Well, maybe we'll come across each other again, but I'm going home now. I'm about ready for retirement."

And we parted company. I went to the chief engineer's office to begin my day's work and Harry (Bob) went to his room, picked up his suitcase, and went over the gangway, and I returned to the boat deck to wave good bye to him.

The only other man I knew in the company who was familiar with his story was Captain John Green, United States Lines Marine Superintendent, to whom I referred earlier.

After the *American Liberty* left New York on its next voyage, I returned to the office and spoke to Green to tell him I had seen "Klitch," and he informed me he knew he was aboard for the one trip, but he had sworn to keep the secret.

Several months later, Green called me to tell me Harry's wife had called to tell him that her husband had passed away a month earlier and she asked him what he thought she should do with her husband's sextant.

"What did you tell her?" I asked.

"I suggested she donate it to the Merchant Marine Academy at Kings Point where it can be used for training young men to become mates."

"Did you suggest she include the story of her husband along with the sextant?"

"Yes, I did, but I don't know if she will."

In retrospect, I found myself angry, perhaps foolishly, because he had not confided in me about his situation on those occasions when we confronted each other, but my feelings were probably more of a selfish nature than anger. After all, because of his gregarious disposition he had befriended hundreds of people during his career and he could have easily been exposed, even unwittingly, by anyone of them, even me!

MISCELLANEOUS

I had an interesting situation happen in Ulsan, Korea, a year later when I had to kill time in my hotel room waiting for the shipyard to get their paperwork together for price negotiations. I was staying in the Diamond Hotel, which was brand new and had all the amenities of any new hotel in the States. It was air conditioned throughout, had an excellent restaurant and bar, and was very comfortable. It had been built by the Hyundai Shipyard to accommodate visiting customers of the yard, as well as customers of the Hyundai automobile plant nearby, and since a great deal of their customer base was Americans, they made it a point to duplicate conditions found in the States.

Once again, the ship had sailed from Korea on Friday and I had to wait until Monday to negotiate the bill. Like so many shipyards in the world, Saturday and Sunday were just two more workdays in the week, so at least I knew I would get the figures on Monday. I received a call from them on Monday at about 11:30 A.M. telling me they would like to get together with me to begin discussing the invoice.

Two men arrived at my room about fifteen minutes later and suggested that because of the noon hour we should go out and enjoy a sumptuous Korean meal and then negotiate. I told them I had just finished a big American-style breakfast, thanked them for the invitation, and suggested they leave the bill with me to look over while they went out for dinner. They agreed to this suggestion, probably realizing it would speed up the settlement bill.

Being a fully air-conditioned hotel, however, had its drawbacks. The windows in my room were sealed closed to prevent anyone opening them, thus upsetting the balance of the air conditioning system. My two weeks there had been quite comfortable because the room temperature was always just right, so I found no need to open a window.

The two men returned in about two hours and knocked on my door. I invited them to sit down at a table I had arranged to have brought in for this purpose because these sessions often ended up with repair lists, time sheets, vendor's invoices, and so forth spread all over the area. I closed the door to my room and then it hit me: these guys had eaten a kimche lunch, a Korean dish made of fermented cabbage, garlic, and other "fragrant" vegetables, and I was a "captive" in the room with them and couldn't even open a window!

The smell was overwhelming, so needless to say we reached an agreement very quickly and they shook hands and left. Afterward, I began to wonder if they had a method to their madness, and on top of that they probably put my name down as having been present at dinner! I then left the room and went to the hotel bar to give the room a chance to air out!

• • •

One of our port captains, Ed Yarborough, told me of an incident which occurred while he was serving as third mate aboard our passenger ship, the SS *Washington*, in 1937. He was standing his watch at midday on the bridge of the vessel which was heading eastbound from New York to Europe when the bow lookout reported what appeared to be a large silver ball sweeping down from the sky and coming toward the ship nearly at sea level at a fast speed!

The term UFO had not been dreamed up at that time as the huge round object kept approaching and closing in on them rapidly. He called the captain and they viewed the object with binoculars as it approached and then realized it was the eight hundred-foot German dirigible *Hindenburg* which had changed its flight pattern to pass closely over the two-stack passenger ship to give the passengers a good look, both on board the ship and the dirigible.

Little did the passengers of either craft realize this would be the last voyage of the *Hindenburg* because it crashed while attempting a mooring at Lakehurst, New Jersey, the following day with a loss of several lives!

EPILOGUE

In 1941, during my senior year in high school in Leicester, Massachusetts, my classmates and I were discussing what lay ahead for us after graduation. War had a pretty good head start in Europe and it was inevitable that our country would soon be a part of it, so the question became "What should we do with our young lives?"

Many of my friends had made their plans; no, not college at this time, not with a war around the corner, but to join the army air corps, become a pilot, and after the war ended, join a major airline as a commercial pilot! I talked to my father about it—he had been a sailor in World War I—and he suggested if I wanted to fight for my country, I should go into the navy.

"You'll always have a bunk to sleep in on board ship," he would say. "If you join the army you'll be sleeping in trenches and they are always muddy," he added, his thoughts going back to 1918.

My older brother had already been admitted to Massachusetts Nautical School, apparently heeding our father's advice. I had no desires about the army air corps, but the Nautical School sounded pretty good. It went through my mind that my classmates would be coming out of flight school as second lieutenants, but I'd be graduating from the Nautical School with an ensign's commission, so at least we'd be equals! To this day, I don't know why that bothered me!

My friends joined the air corps. Two of them became second lieutenants and two were washed out of pilot training and became gunners. All, however, served honorably and came home safely. Upon graduation in 1943 from the Nautical School, whose name was changed to Massachusetts Maritime Academy just as I entered, I had a choice: Apply for active duty with the navy and remain on active duty for the duration of the war plus six months or go to sea in the merchant marine as a third assistant engineer.

At the maritime academy I had taken the marine engineering course and was granted the license as well as my ensign's commission upon graduation.

A representative from the War Shipping Administration had addressed my class prior to graduation and pleaded with us to go to sea in the merchant marine on our license instead of requesting active duty in the navy because of the critical shortage of engineers and mates in the merchant marine, and that many colleges were pumping out "ninety-day wonders" at a rapid rate, so at that point in time the navy was saturated with ensigns.

An added advantage we would have by going to sea in the merchant marine was that we could make one trip and if the life at sea didn't appeal to us, we still had the navy commission to fall back on. Navy active duty held no such alternative.

Most of my classmates and I listened to the pleading of the WSA representative and therefore registered with them and were shipped out on merchant ships within two weeks. At this time President Roosevelt was praising the men of the merchant marine and assured us that we would be granted all the privileges and benefits granted to the members of the armed forces at the end of the conflict.

Sadly, this was not the case, however. When the war ended in Europe and Japan surrendered, the men of the merchant marine were forgotten while GIs enjoyed college tuition relief, reduced mortgage interest rates, hospitalization, and many other benefits. Finally, in 1988, the wartime merchant mariner was recognized and granted veterans' status—forty-three years late! Several of us were extremely upset because had my class applied for active duty in the navy in 1943, we would have been veterans forty-three years earlier and enjoyed the benefits of the GI Bill.

Aside from this, however, going to sea during the war did set up my future because, for lack of any other training except going to sea, I decided to make it a career. I remained with United States Lines (the company with which I had been placed by the War Shipping Administration) for the balance of my working years, retiring in 1986 after forty-three years in the company.

As I stated earlier, I took advantage of an opening on the staff of the superintendent engineer of the company in 1961 and became a port engineer, giving up my seagoing career. I enjoyed going to sea, seeing so many places all over the world, but one advantage a sailor had in those days was the time spent in port. With the break bulk cargo ships in use then, the cargo had to be handled by longshoremen in the cargo hold and on the piers with little mechanical assistance. Cargo would be manually lifted by them and put into cargo nets or on pallets, and each load lifted from the cargo space and landed on the pier. This was time consuming and resulted in many days spent in each port. This not only gave the crew ample time to perform repairs, but plenty of time for shore leave.

Added to this was the location in each city where the ships tied up for cargo operations. Most cities had cargo working piers in the center of the metropolis, a great location for shore leave, sightseeing, etc. Today, with container ship operations the name of the game, shore leave time is at a minimum because of the speed of discharging and reloading containers. Also, most cities have built container terminals miles from the city centers, due to the need for rail facilities and high-speed truck highways for access to the terminals; therefore, it is hardly worth a sailor's time to attempt to go to the city for sightseeing or shopping, not to mention just going out for a "fast beer" across the street!

Today the United States Merchant Marine Academy at Kings Point, New York; Massachusetts Maritime Academy; New York State Maritime College; Maine Maritime Academy; California and Texas Maritime Academies continue to graduate young men and women with licenses for service as merchant marine officers in an industry which has dwindled from a peacetime high in 1950 of nearly 3,500 hundred ships to under 350 in 2001, with a corresponding loss of hundreds of jobs.

In 2001 Massachusetts, for example, graduated fifty-five third assistant engineers and twenty-seven third mates, while the Merchant Marine Academy graduated a total of two hundred eighteen, some with engineer licenses and others as mates, and the other academies' numbers are similar for the same period. While the trend today is for more engineering graduates, with a ratio of two to one, during World War II the reverse was true, with more deck officers graduating than engineers, but with the same ratio. My class had thirteen engineers and twenty-one deck. Not all graduates intend to go to sea today, however. Some enter the military while others go on to college, and still others enter the maritime field in shore positions. Needless to say, the engineering graduate probably has a better shot at a shore position outside the industry than a deck officer because of the nature of his training. Today the lack of available positions aboard ship weighs heavily on the enrollment of the maritime academies; therefore, many schools are opening their ranks to their students in degreed courses offered in facilities and plant engineering, facilities and environment engineering, and marine environmental engineering for survival.

I enjoyed going to sea and working for a steamship company as a career; however, I must add that I was there in its heyday and, as some will say, "during the good old days."

As one wag once said, "The only trouble with being in the good old days is that we were in them and didn't know it!"

GLOSSARY

Navy (regular type)
Merchant Marine (Italics)

Abreast
Alongside, or bearing 90° ahead.
One of two found on most women.

Advance Force
A force preceding the main part toward an objective.
The first guys ashore in a new port.

Bilge
The curved part of a ship's hull where the sides and flat bottom meet.
That section of the engine room which has a sign reading, Don't use this space as a men's room.

Bitter End
The end of the line.
What a sailor's date often comes to when she asks for payment.

Bitts
A pair of iron heads on board ship set vertically in the deck to which mooring lines are made fast.
Two of these are worth twenty-five cents.

Black Gang
That part of a ships' company which comprises the engine department.
That clever group of guys who keep the ship running smoothly.

185

Boom
A spar having many uses.
Noise made when a cannon is fired.

Brow
A portable gangway from a vessel to a pier.
That area of an engineer's forehead which is always sweating trying to please those on the bridge.

Buoys
Floating beacons.
Opposite of gurls.

Camel
A float used as a fender to keep a vessel off a wharf.
A brand of cigarettes sold in the slop chest.

Charley Noble
Galley smokestack
A short smokestack always catching fire due to so much galley grease used in cooking.

Check
To ease off slowly.
What a crew member is paid off in, instead of cash.

Collision Matts
A portable tarpaulin lowered over the side in the event of a collision, to prevent entry of water to ship.
Can be either flapjacks or pancakes, depending on ingredients.

Course
The direction steered by a vessel.
The answer given by an oiler when asked if he pumped the bilges.

Dead Light
A glass lens fitted into a deck or bulkhead for admitting light.
A light bulb that needs changing.

Dip
To lower a flag partway.
Term used by a guy swimming over the side at an anchorage.

Dogs
Small metal fittings used to secure a watertight door.
Names given to ladies of the evening who are not too pretty.

Dog Watch
One of the early watches, two hours long.
Guys standing on the boat deck, watching the above-named ladies strutting on the pier.

Feeling the Way
Slowly proceeding with caution.
Line given to a young lady in a bar.

Fix
Accurate determination of latitude and longitude
Something a guy can be fired for taking.

Fogy
An increase in pay due to longevity.
Any guy over sixty to a guy in his twenties.

Forward
In the direction of the bow.
Something a girl sometimes accuses a guy of being.

Gadget
A name given to an object whose real name is unknown.
Merchant marine cadet.

Garble
An instance of incorrect wording in a message.
Something the purser tells you to do when you have a sore throat.

Glass
Spyglass or barometer.
Something you drink out of.

Half Mast
Position of flag when hoisted halfway.
Where your trousers are during a hernia or short-arm inspection.

Haul
To pull.
In Germany, where beer is served.

Heel
To list over.
Back part of a shoe.

Holiday
An unpainted area.
Day when everyone is paid overtime.

Jack
Flag.
Nickname for John.

Knock Off
To stop doing something.
Time to have a couple of beers.

Knock Up
Unknown in navy lingo.
Should have knocked off sooner.

Lay
Order meaning to go, such as, "Lay aft."
Some are good; some aren't!

Lee
Away from the wind.
The guy General Grant licked.

Line
A piece of rope.
What a guy gives a girl.

Mess
A group of people eating together
Crude name given to some meals aboard ship.

Painter
A line in a small boat for towing.
A guy on the handle of a paintbrush.

Pip
A blip on the radar screen.
One of two which girls have.

Pooped
When the sea breaks over the stern.
What an engineer is after answering a ridiculous number of bells on the telegraph.

Port
The left side of the ship
A nice smooth wine.

Quarters
Living compartments.
Coins, four of which add up to a dollar.

Screw
The propeller.
Same.

Scuttlebutt
Drinking fountain.
Rumors aboard.

Sea Bag
Canvas bag used by sailors when traveling.
Lady of the evening who was smuggled aboard to ply her trade.

Sea Lawyer
A seaman who is prone to argue against authority
Same.

Short Stay
When the ship is brought up on the anchor chain.
A brief visit to a house of ill repute.

Stern
The after end of a ship.
What some seamen say the captain is.

Tompion
A plug inserted into the muzzle of a gun to protect it from foul weather.
Almost the same, but spelled Tampon.

Trick
A period of duty at the steering wheel.
Another name for time spent with a lady of the evening.

Uniform of the day
That uniform prescribed to be worn at a particular time of day.
A touchy subject on merchant ships, depending on the whims of the captain. Always difficult for black gang guys to comply with because of their working conditions.

Vast
An order to halt heaving.
Opposite of slow.

Wheel
Ship's steering wheel.
The propeller.

Watch
A period of time aboard ship.
Something worn on your wrist.

Where Away
A question directed to a lookout reporting a light or ship.
A stupid question I could never understand, even as a cadet!

Wide Berth

Keeping a comfortable distance from ship or shore.

The captain's or chief engineer's bunk on a merchant vessel as compared to those of other officers or crew.